House Beautiful
HOME HANDBOOK

House Beautiful
HOME HANDBOOK

EDITED BY
PAT ROBERTS

WRITTEN AND COMPILED BY
ELIZABETH MARTYN

EBURY PRESS
LONDON

First published in 1992 in Great Britain by Ebury Press
an imprint of the Random Century Group
Random Century House
20 Vauxhall Bridge Road
London SW1V 2SA

British Library Cataloguing-in-Publication Data

A catalogue record for this book is available from the
British Library

ISBN 0 09 175358 9

Designer: Janet James

Typeset in Monophoto Sabon
by Advanced Filmsetters (Glasgow) Ltd
Printed and bound in Great Britain by
Butler and Tanner Ltd, Frome and London

CONTENTS

INTRODUCTION

Anyone who takes pride and pleasure in their home will love this book.

House Beautiful is the award winning magazine with original ideas and know-how for homes large or small. As you turn the pages, you'll find projects both pretty and practical, outlined with expertise and enthusiasm.

The keynote of our Handbook is individuality – no two homes are the same, even if they look identical from the outside. That's why all the imaginative ideas we show are offered as suggestions, and not as dictates on how to decorate rooms and make improvements.

Of course, it isn't possible for me to step inside your home and personalise all our advice, but I can guarantee help with one common aspiration: the search for believable style to make or buy, using just as much time and money as you can afford.

Confidence in colour and co-ordination is the real key to creating a stylish and comfortable home, and inspiration is what everyone needs most. It's here in abundance, in our exciting, first *House Beautiful* book.

Step inside, to a whole world of home ideas.

Pat Roberts

Editor

ONE

ROOMS WITH STYLE

An inspirational room-by-room guide, to help you choose looks you'll love to live with. The important basics are here: buying furniture, organising storage, getting the lighting right. Room planning receives special attention, with hints on maximising every bit of space. And there are masses of ideas for stunning decorating schemes and clever design effects.

It's easy to be tempted by the stylish kitchens on display in the showrooms, but to get the very best from a new kitchen you must plan carefully. First make the basic decisions about equipment, then do some accurate measuring up and start thinking about ways to make use of every bit of available space.

KITCHENS

Drawing up a floor plan

The work triangle

Making the most of space

Brilliant storage ideas

Which work surface?

Where to site appliances

It is vital to take time and care over planning a kitchen. Once your appliances are plumbed and wired in, and the units are in place, it could be virtually impossible to move them and you will have to live with any mistakes.

Arm yourself with a tape measure and some graph paper, and draw up an accurate plan of the room, to scale, indicating places where the floor or walls are not level, or the corners are not square. Mark doors, including the direction in which they open; and windows, including the height to the sill.

Next, decide which appliances you would like to have, and find out their dimensions, including space for wires, pipes and ventilation at the back. Using scaled cut-outs of each appliance, try them in different positions on your plan to see how they fit best. Remember the ideal work triangle of fridge-cooker-sink (see page 14), and bear in mind the various constraints on where items can be placed – see page 15 for guidance. Once you've settled on the positions of the appliances, add cut-outs of the units to complete the plan.

When you're happy with the way your plan works on paper, measure it out carefully in the kitchen or, if you can, mark it on the floor, to make absolutely sure that everything will fit in. Take particular care over appliances and units sited in corners.

Custom-made units can include all sorts of desirable extras, from a knife block to a tiered work surface.

Grainy green paint effect on the doors gives the decor a subtle lift and is far less clinical than plain white.

A made-to-measure wall cabinet butts up to the cornice and provides a useful mix of shelf space and cupboards.

A space for everything

When you are working out how many cupboards you will need, it is helpful to write down everything you want to store in the kitchen, from brooms and mops, down to pots, pans and crockery, electrical items and food. Be as generous as you can: the more storage space you have, the more you seem to need.

Look for a kitchen range which offers flexible and imaginative storage. Carousels which make full use of corner units are very handy, or you can hang open shelves around a corner if there isn't room for a cupboard. Many manufacturers make slim-line units which fit into odd spaces, and have all sorts of drawers, racks, shelves and half-shelves to offer. Never allow cupboard space to go to waste. If you are storing items which don't take up the full height, you might be able to slot in an extra shelf, or a basket which hangs below the shelf.

Rubbish bins are bulky and unattractive. A waste-disposal unit fitted in a sink will gobble up a lot of kitchen waste and enable you to have a smaller bin, tucked neatly out of sight behind a cupboard door.

Valuable drawer space can be freed for less frequently used items, by hanging cooking utensils on wall-mounted racks. Ceiling racks are attractive, but be sure your room is high enough to take one safely. Don't be tempted to keep too many items on permanent display on the worktop. Unless in almost daily use, most things are better stashed away in cupboards where they won't gather dust and grime. Store the most frequently used objects in the most accessible places, and use high and low cupboards and drawers for large or awkwardly shaped equipment which is needed only occasionally.

Choosing cupboards

Cupboards come in a range of standard widths. The narrowest are usually 200 mm wide, increasing in steps of 100 mm up to a maximum of 600 mm for single cupboards and 1200 mm for units with double doors.

Wall cupboards are seldom more than 300 mm deep to allow head room. Floor units can be 500 mm or 600 mm deep. You will need 600 mm deep units to accommodate built-in or built-under appliances. However, if your appliances need complicated piping, 500 mm units could give you a useful gap at the back which can be covered by using a 600 mm deep work surface.

Every scrap of space is used, with floor-to-ceiling cupboards and a wine rack tucked unobtrusively beneath a peninsula breakfast bar.

1 End shelves for storage jars and books.

2 Food storage – fridge etc – should be near to preparation area.

3 Task lighting is provided by strip lights under wall units (you will also need adequate background lighting).

4 600 mm-deep worktop to accommodate large appliances.

5 Double-bowl sink – one bowl taking waste disposal. This

allows working flexibility for washing up, food preparation and use of taps.

6 Sink, washing machine and dishwasher should be sited near to water supply and drainage to simplify plumbing.

7 Corner cupboards contain carousel fitments for easy access.

8 Make sure you have enough power points – usually one double

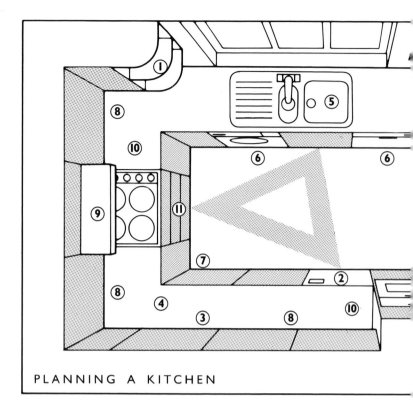

PLANNING A KITCHEN

Choosing work surfaces

Although the standard height is 900 mm, it is sometimes possible to alter this by adjusting a plinth on the base unit to find the height that is most comfortable for you.

Most work surfaces are made of plastic laminate which comes in attractive textured finishes in many different colours. These surfaces are easy to clean, but scratch easily and are not heat-proof. You will need to use chopping boards and trivets to protect them. Wooden worktops are attractive and hardwearing, but expensive. They need re-sealing periodically. Marble and stone can look superb, but are easily stained and very expensive. Ceramic tiles look good and are hardwearing, but it can be difficult to clean the grouting and tiles may crack if heavy objects are dropped on to them.

Look for appliances in smaller than standard widths if you are very pressed for space.

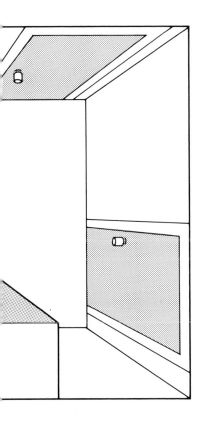

socket for each working area.

9 Cooker hood vented to outside or recirculating if situated on an interior wall.

10 Make sure there is a clear work surface at least 400 mm wide next to the oven and hob.

11 Deep storage drawers under hob.

12 Tall storage for brooms and cleaning materials should not interrupt work surface. Site at end of run.

Where to put appliances

Remember that you will need a power point below the work surface for every large appliance.

Sinks Place on outside wall for easy plumbing. Allow at least 1000 mm for sink and drainer. You will need a minimum of 300 mm of work surface or drainer on both sides of the bowl for stacking washing up. A sink with 1½ or 2 bowls is very useful for preparing food, and you can fit a waste disposal unit into one of the bowls.

Dishwasher Put this as near the sink as you can, both for ease of plumbing and for rinsing crockery.

Washing machine and tumble dryer Choose models that stack to save floor space. Put against an outside wall for plumbing and venting.

Fridge and freezer Position fridge according to the work triangle (see diagram). A separate freezer can be kept elsewhere. Doors can be hinged on left or right, but leave a 100 mm gap next to hinged side so that the door can be opened sufficiently wide to remove the shelves. A nearby work surface of 300 mm or more is useful.

Oven Refer to work triangle (see diagram) for best position of ovens and hobs. Ovens should be kept away from doors for safety and need to be 300 mm away from the nearest corner. You will need at least 400 mm of work surface to one side. Side-opening doors should open away from the work surface.

Hob Keep this away from draughts and curtained windows for safety. Allow 400 mm of work surface on either side. A hob positioned under wall cupboards will need an extractor hood.

Make your bathroom a place to relax in, where you can soothe away your cares in a luxurious bath, or refresh yourself with an invigorating shower. Create a warm atmosphere where you can linger in comfort, and pay attention to tiny details so that the whole look is pulled together.

BATHROOMS

Planning the room

Choosing a suite

Tiles, paper or paint?

Colour schemes

Smart accessorising

All about showers

Baths come in several sizes, so you should be able to find one to fit your space. Small baths are neat, but make sure the tallest member of the family won't feel squashed. A corner bath is a clever solution in a tiny room and children love them, although tall people can't stretch out comfortably for a relaxing soak.

Allow some space between washbasin and WC if you can, otherwise the room will look very cramped. Don't forget to plan wall space for a towel rail near the bath.

Roller blinds in a splash- and steam-proof finish are ideal for bathrooms. Alternatively, choose curtains in a fine fabric to let in maximum light. If your bathroom has no window, you will need a ventilator fan on the wall nearest the taps, and this should be wired to come on automatically with the light.

Acrylic or sealed cork tiles, sisal matting or rubber-backed bathroom carpet are all suitable floorings. Carpet tiles are another possibility and can be replaced in areas which start to look worn.

Left: Swags of flowers add a romantic decorative touch to this luxuriously deep tub.

Right: Soft pinks and greys create a warm, relaxing atmosphere. Generous use of mirrors adds light and an illusion of space.

Choosing a bathroom suite

Baths, made in acrylic, pressed steel or cast iron, are offered in a vast array of colours and designs. Cast iron baths are traditional and very hard-wearing, but they are expensive and very heavy, so check that your bathroom floor can cope with the weight before you buy. Pressed steel is lighter and cheaper than cast iron and wears well. Acrylic baths are cheaper still, but they tend to mark and scratch more easily. Choose a bath with a slip resistant base for safety, especially if you plan to instal a shower over the bath.

White remains the best-selling colour, although there is a revival in neutral shades such as cream. Dark colours can look smart, but show splashes and soap marks and need a lot of cleaning to keep them pristine.

Taps, mixers and shower attachments can be bought separately and there are dozens of different styles, finishes and colours to choose from. Ceramic disc taps are more expensive but because they do away with leak-prone washers, should last for years with no maintenance.

Far right: Serene shades of bluish-grey create a soothing mood. The stainless steel storage unit is not only attractive, but also extremely functional.

Black and white make a striking scheme for a functional modern bathroom. Sunflowers add a vital daub of colour.

Get professionals to fit your new bathroom. A good plumber should be able to replace a WC, washbasin and bath in a couple of days provided the installations are already in place. The job will take longer however, and be more expensive, if you are converting a bedroom and the pipes need re-routing.

Decorating the bathroom

All-over tiling from floor to ceiling is unnecessary, and can make the room feel tomb-like. You'll get a better – and cheaper – effect by tiling the wall nearest the bath and using a water-resistant wallpaper on the other three walls, or painting them with vinyl silk emulsion and adding a wallpaper border.

The cue for the colour scheme will come from the shade of the suite. White is very versatile, and can be combined successfully with soft pastels, bright primaries or dramatic dark colours. Neutrals and pale aqua shades are always popular for walls, and make a small bathroom feel bigger. You can inject colour with towels, blinds and shower curtains.

check point

- A 'country' look, using dried flowers, ornaments etc, can be very pretty in a bathroom, but be prepared for a lot of dusting to keep the effect fresh. Uncluttered, wipe-clean surfaces are easier to care for.

- Co-ordinate accessories to pull the room together. Keep all wood finishes the same, and stick to one or two accent colours right down to little items such as nail brushes and face flannels.

- A glass bowl piled high with unwrapped soaps looks colourful and distinctive.

- Panel the side of the bath with mellow wood to add warmth and interest.

- Keep medicines locked up in one bathroom cabinet, and have another for cosmetics and toiletries.

- Plan decorating so that vital pipes and stopcocks will remain accessible afterwards.

- Remember when planning that a separate WC is a boon, especially with a large family.

- Heated towel rails are an efficient way to keep a bathroom warm. 'Heat'n'light' fitments or plug-in radiators are other widely available options.

SHOWERS

Showers are speedy, invigorating and cheaper to use than baths. The ideal arrangement is to have a separate shower cubicle, or a tiled alcove, with the controls outside. If you lack the space or the money for this option, you can fit a shower over a bath, which should have a wide, flat bottom, preferably non-slip. Surrounding walls should be tiled up to the ceiling and the gap between bath and wall sealed with waterproof sealant. The shower can be screened with a curtain, glass or acrylic screen or a waterproof blind, which can be let down as needed and rolled up neatly out of sight into its container when dry.

Take a shower in the old-fashioned way with this handsome Edwardian hand-held fitting. A free-standing bath is a luxury well worth considering in a large bathroom.

If you are having a new shower installed, employ a qualified plumber and electrician to do the job for you. Choose a shower which includes a thermostatic control to maintain the water temperature regardless of fluctuations when a tap is turned on elsewhere in the house.

In order to operate well, most showers require a 'head' of 1.5 m (5 ft) between the bottom of the water tank and the shower outlet. If the 'head' in your house is less than this, or if the tank is below the shower (if the shower is in a loft conversion, for instance), you will have to fit a pump to circulate the water. You can also use a pump if you want to fit a power shower with more than one shower head, but take professional advice before you do so, as a badly designed system can cause problems.

check point

Which showerhead?

Pulsator jets spit out bullets of high-pressure water rather than a continuous stream. Good for body tone, but not very relaxing.

Needle jets give thin streams of water at piercingly high pressure. Not recommended.

Aerated sprays produce soft streams of water that feel like bathing in silk.

Body jets spray from the walls the whole height of the body. Adjustable sprays are useful, to accommodate people of different heights.

Torrent sprays produce a heavy column of water, like standing under a waterfall.

Multi-mode heads offer a combination of the above sprays by moving a lever or twisting a nozzle. Kids can't reach them though, and they are prone to limescale problems.

An awkwardly shaped corner is transformed into a shower by using cleverly angled glass screens.

It's almost impossible to have too much storage space. With a bit of clever improvisation you can squeeze extra storage into any spare scrap of room in the house.

STORAGE

Few homes have enough storage space. If you are furnishing from scratch and can afford it, it's well worth getting estimates from manufacturers not just of fitted kitchens, but of fitted bedrooms and bathrooms as well, who could provide you with cleverly designed storage to cater for all your needs, even within a limited space. But if your budget won't stretch that far, there are plenty of practical alternatives.

Try not to let any potential storage space go to waste. The back of a cupboard door, for instance, could make a home for ties and belts; small tools; scissors and string. Make good use of hooks, hangers, racks and wire hanging grids in places like these. Often, space is wasted beneath shelves in cupboards. Wire baskets which hang below shelves can be useful for storing tea towels, table linen, stationery and many other items. Keep clutter to a minimum and tidy objects away immediately after use.

Everything a baby needs is kept tidily out of sight behind a curtain.

check point

Top: Handy shelves over a student's desk are jollied up by painting in cheerful primaries.

Above: This seat built into an alcove doubles as a useful blanket box.

● Identify exactly what it is that you need to store. This could range from linen, to books, to children's toys.

● Look at how you can use any available or wasted space to its best advantage. An obvious area to exploit is the space under the stairs.

● Corners are often wasted, but with a little extra planning, shelves made to fit into alcoves can be designed to continue around a corner on to the facing wall. A corner cupboard might make use of wasted space on a landing or in a hallway.

● Freestanding shelving units can occupy valuable wall space where you would rather site a radiator or sofa. Building your own shelving is relatively easy and it can be custom-designed to fit into limited or awkward spaces which would otherwise be redundant.

● The wall space above doors and windows is rarely used. If you are building shelves, consider continuing them around a door or window.

● A display shelf running around a room at picture-rail height is decorative and provides somewhere to keep books or china.

● Choose dual-purpose items of furniture whenever you can. A blanket box can double as a seat or coffee table. Some beds have built-in storage drawers underneath.

First and foremost, decide on the best way to use the space you have. Whether you eat in a huge dining room or a tiny corner of the kitchen doesn't matter, but what is important is to provide a well-chosen table and chairs, adequate storage and suitable lighting. Likewise, living areas need comfortable seats, places to put cups and books, flexible lighting and an air of relaxation.

LIVING & DINING
r o o m s

Capitalising on space

Sofas • Tables • Chairs

Colour schemes

Storage needs

Focal points

Caring for china and glass

Although there is a move back to using separate rooms for living and dining, homes often lack the space to make this possible. For many people, meals are eaten in a dining area, which may be part of the living room, or the kitchen.

There's no reason why a living and dining area cannot co-exist happily in the same room. If you have an older or larger house, it may be possible to have dividing doors between the areas, or you could separate them with a folding screen. Clever lighting is another way to help to shift the emphasis (see page 36).

Think carefully about the activities which will take place in the room, as these should be catered for in the choice of furnishing and decor. Is it a place for rumbustious children's play, or somewhere for adults to escape and relax in front of the TV? Do you need a quiet place for studying or reading? It's often better to put study areas in a more peaceful part of the house, such as a landing or bedroom. Will you want to use a corner of the room for hobbies or sewing? If so, make sure you can work undisturbed and have space to store everything you will need nearby. Perhaps you occasionally have to turn part of the room into a guest bedroom. You'll need a comfortable sofa bed, as well as suitable lighting and storage.

A handsome mirror, a superb fireplace and a strategic vase of flowers together create an irresistible focal point in a room that has a plain and simple decor.

Single chairs provide flexible seating and allow an open view of the glorious roaring fire. Pools of gentle light enhance the cosy mood.

Above right: An octagonal table will seat six happily and can accommodate more at a squeeze. Trailing greenery and richly ruched blinds soften the otherwise stark surroundings.

Seating selection

Before you set foot in a furniture showroom, take careful measurements of your room, doorways and hall to make sure the items you choose will fit into your home. It's helpful to take along a few snaps of your room to remind you of shapes and colours.

When you choose furniture, opt for comfort and quality as well as good looks. Sit on chairs and sofas to find out if they give adequate support and if you can sit right back in them while still keeping your feet flat on the floor. Are the arms the right height for reading or knitting comfortably? Does the shape allow you to stretch out or curl up snugly?

Quality will be dictated by your budget. All new furniture should have flame-retardant upholstery, and it's a good idea to look for burn- and stain-proofed covers. Press the cushions to see if they spring back into shape well – if not, they could soon look flat and worn. If you have young children, go for sturdy, stable furniture with zip-off washable covers and choose patterns rather than plain colours. Removable 'sleeves' save wear on upholstered

Decorating hints

● Practicality is vital, especially if you have children. Steer clear of delicate wallpapers or paints that mark easily.

● Find a starting point such as a rug, curtain fabric or even a picture, and pick your other colours to match.

● Select no more than two or three colours, and base your scheme round tones of these.

● Whites and creams are always popular for ceilings and paintwork, and are good for linking areas of colour and pattern. Bright, dark colours such as ochre and navy can look good on paintwork and make an interesting change from white. They need to be applied with a steady, practised hand, however, as every slip will show.

● Neutrals are soothing and needn't be boring if you liven them up with splashes of strong, warm colour. And it's easy to alter the emphasis later on, if you feel like a change.

● Hang pictures lower than usual in a living room, because people will look at them from a seated position.

● Don't mix different wood finishes. Choose all dark, or all pale, for a co-ordinated room.

arms. If you intend to smarten your furniture up with lots of cushions, pick cushion-covers which are reversible.

A couple of two-seater sofas, or one small sofa and several individual chairs, can be more flexible than a three-piece suite. Larger sofas are lovely for lounging on if you have the space, but bear in mind that sitting in the middle is always awkward.

Tables and dining chairs

If you are very short of space, choose a 'gate-leg' table, which folds down to a slim size when not in use, or go for a small table with one or more extension leaves. Glossy polished wood looks marvellous, but has to be protected with a table cloth or large mats at every meal, and is not suitable to use for hobbies where it might get scratched or marked. Even woods such as sealed oak or pine show marks from hot plates and wet glasses. Candle wax is another hazard. Always stand candlesticks on a mat to prevent drips marking the table. If practicality is your main concern, go for a tough laminate table top – white always looks good.

Choice of shape will be determined by the size of your room. Round tables are useful because there are no 'wasted' corners and everyone can reach the middle of the table, but they take up a lot of space, and cannot be pushed against a wall. Check the spacing of legs and struts when you choose a table. If badly positioned, these could limit your seating arrangements.

There's no reason why your chairs have to match the table – or each other – exactly. You might be able to pick up bargains at a junk shop and strip or paint them to match your scheme. Do check that they are the right height for your table before you buy. Upholstered dining chairs can be useful elsewhere in the house as occasional seating. Whatever you choose, always make sure that your dining chairs are comfortable and offer sufficient support to sit on for a whole evening.

Storage and display

A sideboard is a practical addition to a dining area, as not only can it store cutlery, glass and linen, but the top can be used for serving. Modern designs are narrow enough not to dominate the room. The living area will need shelves and cupboards for books and records (see Storage, page 22 for ideas). One or two low tables near the main seating area are essential, and a round draped table (available cheaply from DIY stores – add your own cover) looks pretty as well as being functional.

Arranging the furniture

If your room has a natural focal point such as a fireplace, you can arrange your seating around this, but place chairs and sofas at angles, rather than blocking the view from the rest of the room. Otherwise, place seating units at right angles or facing each other, and add low tables as needed.

Take into account the main routes between the door and different areas of the room. It is very irritating if people have to walk between the sofa and the TV, say, to get from the dining area to the door.

Dining chairs can be tucked neatly out of sight under the table, or used elsewhere in the room if needed. Disguise the table with a long cloth, or fold it away when not in use.

Ladder-back carver chairs with upholstered seats make for dining in comfort. The bleached-look wood is limed oak, which has a paler finish than traditional oak, and the table, shown fully extended, can lose a central leaf to become the right size for a meal for two or four.

check point

Choosing china and glass

If buying items separately, purchase a few extras in case of breakages. Check that items are dishwasher-safe and avoid metallic trims if you plan to use china in the microwave.

Earthenware is ideal for everyday use, is dishwasher safe, and comes in an enormous range of shapes and designs. Cookware can be used in the freezer and microwave.

Stoneware is tougher than earthenware. It can be used in the dishwasher and can go straight from freezer to the microwave (on defrost).

Porcelain comes in elegant designs, but is tough enough for regular use.

Lead crystal glassware is made by traditional methods, is thin and clear and rings when tapped. It may be decorated with cut or engraved designs.

Soda lime glassware is machine made, tougher than crystal and comes in a wide range of styles for all uses.

Aim for a spacious effect that will make a welcoming impact on everyone who comes to your front door. Light, both natural and artificial, is all-important for an airy feel, and vital for safety on stairs. Crafty decorating tricks can minimise awkward proportions effectively. Keep furniture to a minimum and find ways to fit in unobtrusive storage.

Give any outstanding feature maximum impact by keeping everything around it low key.

HALLS
and stairs

Coping with clutter

Furnishing essentials

Stairs • Spirals • Banisters

Light and space

Storage suggestions

Clever disguises

The hallway is an important part of your home. Not only does it make an immediate impression on anyone who visits, but it is also the link between all other rooms. It can also end up looking bitty, unless, when decorating, you treat the entire area of hall, stairs and landings as one 'room'.

Making an entrance

Unless your hall is huge, keep it fairly clear of furniture. Remember that its main function is as a corridor, and people should not have to negotiate their way round tables and chairs to get from A to B. However, if you can find the space, it is very useful to have a small table, or perhaps a bench, where you can dump keys, shopping and other paraphernalia as you come in.

If you decide to keep your phone in the hall it's helpful to have a firm surface for writing on – a tiny table or shelf would do, but keep a notepad and pen always in place – and even better if you can find room for a chair.

Coats, hats, boots and brollies all find a home in the hall, but a mass of hanging garments can look unattractive. House them in a cupboard, or tuck them out of sight round a corner or in an alcove. Provide more coat hooks than you think you could possibly need, or use a bentwood hatstand or a junk-shop hall-stand. Boots and shoes can be stowed neatly in a big basket or on a wooden rack, and umbrellas kept handy in a suitable container – a coal scuttle or even an old milk churn would do.

Other essentials in the hall are a light switch just inside the front door, a mirror for last minute checks, and a large doormat, preferably recessed to the same level as other flooring.

A spiral with solid steps
can feel safer than one
with open treads.

Far right: Two
complementary
geometrical patterns are
linked by continuing the
black band which borders
the stair carpet round the
edge of the floor tiles.

Upstairs, downstairs

If you are doing up an old house, it can be tempting to rip the stairs out and replace them in a different position. Seek advice from an architect and your local authority before you start wielding a crowbar, however, as staircases are a vital part of the structure and there are many rules and regulations governing alterations to them.

In a house where space is at a premium, you could consider installing a spiral staircase. Bear in mind that it is difficult to negotiate large items of furniture up a spiral. If you do choose one, make sure that there is a handrail, or the steps are covered in a non-slip material rather than a shiny wood finish.

Staircases can feel dark and cramped, especially if they are blocked in. Introduce a lighter feel with banisters, available from DIY stores as a replacement set, complete with handrail.

Decorating themes

Carry the same scheme through the hall and up the stairs to the landing. Pale colours add space and light, although in a large hall you can get away with darker, more dramatic shades. Patterned papers disguise signs of wear and tear and add interest to an area which may not have much furniture. Be careful when mixing patterns that the effect isn't overpowering, and, if in doubt, stick to a combination of one pattern with one or two plain colours. The hall and stairs come in for a lot of wear and tear, so whatever you choose, go for durable finishes which are easy to clean and won't show the odd scuff mark.

The same goes for the flooring. Pick a tough carpet and choose a small, discreet pattern for practicality, rather than a plain colour. Large patterns on the floor will make the hall look smaller. Alternatively, you could sand the boards (see page 96) and add carpet runners (but make sure they are safely secured on the stairs). Sisal or rush matting are hardwearing and inexpensive for a country-look hall; traditional black and white tiles are durable and look superb in the right setting; or you could go for washable vinyl or sealed cork tiles.

Make sure that lighting is bright and well-positioned both in halls and on stairs. Avoid low-wattage fittings or ornate shades that mask the light, and check that corners and the tops and bottoms of stairs are particularly well-lit.

If your hall or stairs boast a window, you might prefer to leave it bare in order to enjoy the maximum light. Otherwise, choose a simple blind if the window is in a main 'traffic' area. An out-of-the-way window could be given a more elaborate treatment which would also introduce softness and colour.

Space savers

Make maximum use of the cupboard under the stairs. You could convert it into a study or sewing area if you're not disturbed by the clatter of people using the stairs over your head. Otherwise, paint it white, fit a light and lots of shelves and use for general

Far right: Glass doors allow light from the sitting room to filter out into the hall. Quarry tiles make a sturdily practical floor.

A small, snug sofa; a handy table; some shelves: this hall cleverly uses every available space, without looking overcrowded.

storage. Make sure that meters and stopcocks are still accessible – it may be possible to move meters outside the house. Freezers can be difficult to get at under the stairs, and it might be more sensible to put laundry equipment there, if you can alter the plumbing. You might even be able to squeeze in a tiny cloakroom.

Bookshelves can look good on a landing and there might also be room for a blanket chest. The landing can be a good spot for a little home office: a hinge-down desk top, a shelf or two for files, a phone extension and folding chair are all you need. If a large airing cupboard is cluttering up your landing, consider installing a combination boiler, which does away with the need for a hot water tank, and can be sited high up on the wall.

check point

Optical illusions

Ceiling too high

● Paint ceiling a darker colour than the walls, finishing at picture-rail height. Conceal 'join' with a border.
● In a dark hall, hang several low pendant lights, to draw the eye down.
● Add interest lower down the wall by adding a dado rail, or painting an existing rail in a dark or bright colour. Or hang a wallpaper border at dado height, and use different colours or patterns above and below.

Hall too small

● Be ruthless about clutter.
● Use pale colours and small patterns.
● Have banisters rather than blocked-in stairs.
● Use light coloured carpet in hall and on stairs.

Hall too narrow

● Take flooring across the full width of the hall.
● Pick a horizontally striped carpet, or lay tiles in a horizontal pattern.

Hall too dark

● Choose light colours and use white for ceilings and paintwork.
● As well as good background lighting, fit wall uplighters at intervals to create extra pools of light.
● A collection of mirrors hung together help to maximise available light.

Lighting can make or break your design scheme. It highlights or disguises the room's features, defines its colours and contours, and generally helps to create the background mood. Here's how to make light work in your home.

LIGHTING

L ighting is often the hardest thing to get right in interior design. The conventional arrangement of a central pendant fitted with a tungsten filament bulb, gives out an indiscriminate glare that illuminates all corners of the room. Better by far to choose a whole range of freestanding uplighters, table and standard lamps and directional desk and work lamps, and position them freely to give the effect you want, where you want it.

If you get the chance, have some 5-amp sockets fitted around the room for lamps, which will be linked to the main light switch. This means that you only need to turn one switch to illuminate all the lamps in the room. Make the main switch a dimmer so you can control the amount of light you need.

● **Exploit texture** The angle of light is crucial: a beam of light that just grazes the brickwork above an open fireplace will reveal its rough texture. Light it straight on, and it will just look dull.

● **Use dimmers** An easy way to vary the mood.

● **Create accents** Focus light on a beautiful object to produce a sense of drama. Use spotlights, wall lights and downlights and experiment with the position of objects.

● **Vary positions** Create pools of light at different heights with uplighters, table lamps and wall-fixed lights.

● **Think practically** Table and standard lamps can easily be knocked over by small children, so position them where they are least vulnerable, and have fixed light sources as well.

Far left: Swivel-head spotlights can be trained on to any feature for extra impact.

Left: A beautifully simple standard which creates a soft glow of background light.

37

Choosing fittings

So how do you go about deciding what to use, where? A lot will depend on the style of your room, and also the way it is used. Most rooms need three types of lighting: general lighting, which provides background light for the whole room; task lighting, which gives a pool or beam of light for reading or sewing; and effect lighting, which picks out areas, or features such as pictures and plants, which you want to accent.

General lighting Pendant lights suspended from the ceiling are simple and cheap, but can create shadows or give too much light. Downlights recessed into the ceiling give a very discreet light which, because the beams shine straight down and the bulbs are hidden, does not cause any glare. However, they are expensive to install, and may have to be concealed in a false ceiling.

Spotlights, either fixed, or moveable along a ceiling track, are much easier to install. They can be angled to bounce the light off walls or ceiling, or to shine on to an important area such as a

You can use a variety of light sources in a room to create a warm mood or a dramatic effect.

kitchen worktop. It can be tricky to arrange them so that they don't glare into your eyes, however.

Halogen generates a great amount of light from a tiny bulb, and comes close to natural daylight. You can use it in an uplighter to reflect off the ceiling and provide enough light for the whole room. Halogen bulbs can only be used in special fittings, however, which do not fit in with all types of decor.

Task lighting Position task lights carefully, so that they do not create shadows on your work. Consider desk lamps, clip-on spotlights and adjustable floor-standing lamps in this category, and if possible, place them so they shine over your shoulder. Many task lights are very flexible and are fitted to swivel arms.

Effect lighting Table lamps can be used to give soft pools of light to add interest to a room. Uplighters, downlighters and spotlights can all be used to emphasise decorative objects, or just to create pleasing patches of light.

1 Use a picture light to draw attention to a favourite painting.

2 If you fit a rise-and-fall lamp in a dining area, you can bring it down to create an intimate pool of light when entertaining friends, but still have the option of using it as a general-purpose pendant light.

3 For desks and work areas, use task lighting to make sure you have a powerful source of light which you can direct straight onto the job in hand, like this traditionally shaped desk lamp.

4 Table lamps create warm pools of light and are also decorative – you could always match the shade to your soft furnishings.

5 Try a wall uplighter instead of a central pendant. Light washes the walls and bounces off the ceiling, creating effective areas of shadow.

Every age group has different needs from a bedroom. Adults want a quiet haven where they can retreat, children need space to play, while teenagers might be studying or entertaining friends. Don't neglect the essentials though: everyone needs flexible storage, a comfortable bed and bedding that's cosy and practical.

Navy and cream make an unusual and very sophisticated choice. Mellow ochre on the walls provides warmth.

BEDROOMS

Soothing colours

Buying beds and mattresses

Duvets and pillows

Storage solutions

Nurseries

Children • Teenagers

A bedroom is more than just a place to sleep, it is also somewhere to unwind, to grab a few moments of peace, to relax with your partner or to enjoy a quiet read. What's more, there's no need to follow the strictly practical approach which has to come first in the rest of the house. You can indulge in delicate fabrics and wallpapers, and use pale colours to your heart's content.

Creating a restful room

The bedcover inevitably plays an important part in the room because of its size, and you could use it as a starting point for your decorating scheme. Flowery designs offer scope to pick up the floral theme in a smaller – or larger – version on curtains, adding plain or striped walls and pulling everything together with a flowered border. Or you might prefer a bold pattern on the bedcover, picking out the colours in simpler designs elsewhere. There are dozens of ways to mix and match fabrics, wallcoverings and carpets, so look around at the many co-ordinated ranges available for inspiration.

Soft colours are more soothing than primaries. To give your bedroom a bright, sunny feel – regardless of the weather – go for light yellow, pinky peach or honey beige. If, however, you regard your bedroom as an after-dark retreat, you could create a warm and inviting colour scheme using crimsons and midnight blue, or warm shades of terracotta and rich cream.

Lighting is very important in the bedroom. Wall lights can produce romantic pools of soft light on the walls, and you will also need individual bedside lamps. You should have a good source of light, angled to shine on to your face, for applying make

check point

Choosing bedding

Quilts and duvets are light, warm and make bed-making a breeze. A wide selection of types and sizes is available under the 'Fogarty' label. *Tog* The tog number measures the amount of warmth retained by the quilt. As a guide, if your bedroom is well heated, a 9.0 or 10.5 tog quilt will be warm enough, but in a chillier room, or if you like to be extra-warm in bed, choose a 12.0 or 13.5 tog quilt.

Duvets are filled with duck or goose down and/or feathers. Pure down is lightest and softest of all. These fillings breathe during the night, to dispel body moisture. Duvets are not usually washable.

Quilts are filled with man-made fibres. Like duvets, they come with different tog ratings. Being washable, they are ideal for children.

Pillows Choose pillows that will stay firm enough to support your head and neck properly, all night. Pillows are available filled with down and down-and-feather mixtures, and with less expensive man-made fillings.

Blankets Wool blankets are light and warm, and breathe naturally, but are expensive. Blankets in man-made fibres wear well and are warm, but can make sleepers feel too hot, since they don't breathe in the same way as wool.

The predominant colours in this scheme are taken from the bedcover. Cushions, lamps, vases and picture trims add to the overall effect.

up. A full-length mirror is also invaluable, and should be positioned carefully so that you can see yourself clearly both in daylight and artificial light.

Window treatments can be simple or extravagant, depending on the mood of the rest of the room. Unlined cotton curtains will let some daylight filter through, but won't insulate against the cold as effectively as heavier, lined curtains.

Furnishing the bedroom

Always buy the best bed you can afford and don't be afraid to lie on the bed in the showroom to make sure that it is comfortable and to establish how firm a mattress you want.

Bed bases There are three types of base. *Firm-edge* has a wooden frame, and is useful if the bed is to be used as a seat during the day. *Sprung-edge* has springs right up to the edge, is more expensive but should last longer. *Wooden* bases are cheaper and wear well. Slats should be well-spaced for ventilation and, on a double bed, should have a lengthways support to prevent sagging.

Mattresses *Pocket-sprung* are the best, especially for partners of different weights, as each spring reacts individually to the weight placed upon it. The more springs in the mattress, the better it is. *Open-sprung* mattresses are cheaper, but the springs are inter-linked and will tend to sag towards the heavier partner. *Foam* mattresses are useful for people who suffer from dust allergies, but a good quality one can be as expensive as a sprung mattress.

Storage Fitted storage units can make maximum use of the space available and look very neat. However, if you are planning to move house in future, it might be better to choose free-standing furniture which you can take with you. Some ranges are designed to look 'built-in'. A cheaper, DIY alternative, is to fit sliding doors across an alcove to turn it into a wardrobe. Fit a hanging rail and wire baskets for items that need to be stored folded and add a high-level shelf to store suitcases.

A blanket box tucked in under a window provides a useful seat as well as a place to stow bulky bedding. And make valuable use of the 'lost' space under the bed, and buy a bed with storage drawers in the base.

Children's rooms

Practicality and planning are the key-notes here. Choose furniture and decorating materials with an eye to durability and safety (see pages 126–129), and bear in mind that the room must 'grow' at the same rate as the child.

Nurseries You may fall in love with a pretty wallpaper design, but babies turn into sticky-fingered toddlers very quickly. A tough vinyl that can stand up to scribbling and scrubbing is ideal, or you could paint the walls with a washable vinyl silk. Colourful extras can add character to the room: bright curtains or a roller blind with a matching frieze, gaily painted furniture. You will need a chest of drawers to store baby clothes, toys and bits and pieces; and a flat surface, preferably at work-top height, for nappy-changing. A dim night light is invaluable for late night feeds in the early days, and will still be useful later on.

Growing up A cot will soon need to be replaced with a full-sized single bed. Families where children share a room may find bunk beds useful. Provide each child with a separate reading lamp, and ensure that the design allows enough head-room for the occupant of the bottom bunk to sit up and play.

Let your child have a say in the decoration of the room. He or she will get a lot of pleasure from a wallpaper or duvet cover patterned with a favourite children's character. Alternatively, a

A versatile storage idea for a teenager's room. Bold colours make a practical feature decorative as well.

border featuring the hero or heroine of the moment can be used on a plain wall, and a different border pasted on top later on.

As the child gets older, he or she will need lots of storage space for toys: a roomy cupboard, a wooden or wicker chest, or even an alcove filled with shelves and screened with a roller blind. Fitted storage units can solve a lot of problems, but be sure that shelves and other fittings can be moved up as the child becomes taller. One or two extra power points are bound to come in useful.

Teenage years A well-lit desk top and some bookshelves are essentials for the teenager who is grappling with homework. The bedroom could also become a place for listening to music, watching TV or using a home computer, although parents may have to introduce some rules about hours of use, volume etc. If two young people are sharing a room, it's helpful to provide them with some privacy. You might be able to fit a room divider, which could be a simple curtain, or introduce separate colour schemes to mark out each persons' 'territory'.

Bears, bears everywhere – but not so many that the effect is overwhelming. A crisp blue and white gingham check makes an effective, simple contrast.

TWO

CREATING A BEAUTIFUL HOME

The colours and patterns you choose for walls, windows and floors can make an enormous difference to the mood of each room. You can produce an atmosphere that's warm and peaceful or bright and busy, just by changing the shade of the paint, or the wallpaper design. To get your eye in, build up a collection of pleasing swatches and samples, and browse through books, magazines and catalogues regularly for inspiration.

Paint is versatile, easy to apply and comes in a rainbow of colours. There are finishes to suit walls, woodwork and ceilings, and a vast range of shades from brilliant primaries to barely-there pastels. Once you've learned the basics you can go on to create different moods with special paint effects.

PAINT

Giving a room a fresh coat of paint is a quick and relatively inexpensive way to decorate and, by choosing the colour carefully, can make a dramatic difference to the atmosphere and appearance. For the best results, however, you should spend some time preparing the surfaces to be painted.

Getting ready

Painted walls and ceilings which are already in good condition should be washed with paint cleaner or sugar soap, then rinsed well. Old paintwork which is cracking or flaking should be removed with a scraper. Use filler to make good any cracks or holes, then sand down until the surface is smooth.

You may be able to paint over sound wallpaper, but make sure that it is very firmly stuck to the wall, particularly where the paper joins. Try the paint on a small patch first. Some colours, especially gold, show through paint and can't easily be covered.

Left: Cool lilac makes a soothing backdrop which complements the raspberry-ripple fabric. A neat pink border ties in with the curtain colour.

Right: Soft apricot is an imaginative and refreshing partner for the more sombre tones of carpet and furniture.

Paint quantities

● To estimate how much paint to buy, first measure the area of the walls of the room. There's no need to subtract anything for doors or windows, simply multiply the height and width of each wall and add the areas together to get the total for the room.

● The quantity you need will depend on the type of paint you are using, and the surface to be covered.

● Most manufacturers provide a coverage guide on the can, and the table below gives approximate amounts.

● Porous surfaces will soak up more paint than non-absorbent surfaces.

● If you are painting a pale colour over a dark one, you may need to use more coats than you would to apply a dark colour over a pale one.

● Try to buy all the paint at the same time, as batches may vary slightly.

Approx coverage per litre of paint

Type of paint	sq m
Undercoat	11
Non-drip gloss	13
Vinyl silk emulsion	14
Vinyl matt emulsion	15

Tools for the job

Brushes You will need narrow ones for edges, and wider ones if you decide to paint the main area with a brush. Cheap brushes don't wear well and tend to shed bristles, but are usually inexpensive enough to throw away when the job is done. More expensive brushes will last for years, but only if you clean them meticulously after every use.

Rollers and pads Rollers are quick to use and, with practice, produce a good finish. Buy nylon, lambswool or mohair rather than cheaper foam. You will need a paint tray as well. Pads are very easy to use, but they are not as quick as rollers, nor do they produce such a smooth result.

All in order

You can make life a lot simpler by following the correct working sequence when painting a room. Start with the ceiling, beginning nearest the window. Work in daylight if you can, as it's very hard to see what you are doing by artificial light, especially if you are applying a new coat of the same colour.

Once the ceiling is done, move on to the walls. Don't start a wall unless you can finish it in the same session. Begin in the top right-hand corner and paint in horizontal strips across the complete width of the wall. Be careful when painting around light switches that no paint dribbles down behind them. Ideally, switch the power off at the mains before starting. Use a special angled brush to get behind radiators.

Leave painting woodwork until all the walls are complete. Do windows first thing in the morning, so that they are as dry as possible before you shut them at night. Paint other woodwork in the room using the following sequence: doors, picture rails, dado, skirting boards.

Right: Discreetly different shades of green are used to create an unobtrusive frame for this pleasingly symmetrical effect.

Above: Using Chinese-lacquer red in a gloss finish adds exactly the right note of oriental extravagance to this bold colour scheme. The shiny surface produces fascinating reflections from candle flames and lighting, and enhances the exotic mood.

Guide to paint types

All paints fall into one of two categories: *gloss* paints are oil-based and soluble with white spirit; *emulsion* paints are water soluble.

Liquid gloss Very shiny finish. Needs undercoat. Seal bare wood with primer. Mainly used for wood and metal.

Non-drip gloss High-shine finish. Gel-like texture, doesn't drip or run. No undercoat needed. Prime bare wood. Use for wood and metal, good for plastic gutters and drainpipes.

Self-undercoating gloss Combines qualities of liquid and non-drip gloss. Has a thick, creamy consistency, dries to high-shine finish. Covers most colours with a single coat. For wood, metal, plastic.

Mid-sheen oil-based paints Soft-sheen finish. Less tough and harder to keep clean than gloss. No undercoat needed. Usually needs two or more coats. Prime bare wood. May be sold as eggshell or satinwood. Use on walls, woodwork or metal.

Vinyl silk emulsion Silky, low-sheen finish. No undercoat needed. Good for damp, steamy walls in kitchens and bathrooms. Wipes clean. Emphasises flaws, but good for relief-pattern wall coverings. For walls and ceilings.

Vinyl matt emulsion Soft, matt finish. No undercoat needed. Helps disguise uneven surfaces. For walls and ceilings.

Solid emulsion/Roller paint Matt and silk finishes. No undercoat needed. Comes ready packaged in paint tray. Limited range of colours. For walls and ceilings. Doesn't drip or run.

White and discreet bluish-grey make a harmonious scheme that's restful and refreshing.

Colour scheming made easy

Use these guidelines and Colour Code overleaf to choose the best combination of colours for every room in the house.

● Always find a starting point. This may be an existing carpet, sofa or curtains; or could be something as small as a vase or a picture which you particularly like.

● Choose fabrics, carpets and upholstery before you start decorating. They are much more expensive and harder to choose than paint, and cannot be changed as easily.

● Before ordering anything, collect swatches and samples of fabrics that you like. Look at them all together in the room where they are to be used, both in daylight and under artificial light. This is important, because colours change depending on the light in

which you view them, and the way they look in the shop will rarely be the same as the way they look in your home.

● When choosing expensive items such as upholstered furniture and carpets, make sure they are in patterns or colours you feel really comfortable with, as you will probably not want to change them for quite a few years. It is worth bearing in mind that even though you will be keeping those items you may want to change your colour scheme in later years, so check that your patterns are adaptable and not too limiting in terms of what will go with them.

● If you are decorating on a very tight budget and cannot afford to make many major changes, paint is the easiest and cheapest way to give your room a facelift. Alternatively, you could try changing the emphasis in the room by adding an accent colour.

Subtlety is the key to this restful scheme, a delicate interplay of greenish-yellow walls and yellowish-green mantelpiece and alcove seat. Coral accessories add a warming flicker of colour.

53

Troubleshooting

Here are a few painting pointers which could turn a full-blown disaster into a minor mistake.

● To avoid mishaps in the first place, try out your chosen colour before you begin decorating. Small sampler pots of paint come complete with a built-in brush and give you enough paint to try out two coats of colour on an area about 30 cm square (1 sq ft).
● Remember, paint dries a slightly different colour. What looks overpowering when wet may mellow as it dries.
● Add a border. Hanging a wallpaper border is quick and easy, and a small amount of pattern removes some of the emphasis from the walls. Choose one which picks up the paint and fabric colours.
● Sponge or wash over the top with another colour. Sponging tones down the base coat, still allowing it to show through. If your base coat is too pale, beef it up by sponging over it in a slightly darker shade. If the base is too dark, paint a wash over it using white or a paler shade of the base colour.
● Change the emphasis by adding an accent colour for cushions, lampshades, china and other accessories. If your wall colour is too dark, the accent colour should be a bright or pastel colour. If too pale, use a strong accent to catch the eye and distract attention from the walls.

Right: Gentle shades of peach and green make a room which feels light and spacious.

Far right: A study in blue – dragging gives the paint finish a faintly striped appearance, while white bands emphasise the pretty curved shape.

Colour code

Devising a colour scheme for your home should be a pleasure, but instead fills many people with dread. We tend to stick to safe and rather uninspiring colours. But discovering colours that work well together is an adventure in itself. Start a scrapbook to record successful combinations you notice. Collect postcards, pictures from magazines, samples of wallpaper and snippets of fabric. Flowers are miniature colour schemes in themselves, with varying hues within one petal: an almost failsafe approach to colour scheming for your home is to combine several shades of one colour. Or consider how well flowers of different colours can be massed together in a vase. Holiday snaps can provide inspiration too. Think of the combinations of terracotta, white and blue on Greek houses, or the faded pinks and yellows of Italy and the South of France. The splashy contrast of the rape crop against a summer sky; the greens and golds of changing autumn leaves: look around to discover the natural colour combinations of everyday life.

Choosing the mood

Colours can have a powerful effect on your state of mind. Decide what feelings and activities you want each room to encourage and which aspects of your personality you want emphasised, and choose your colour schemes accordingly.

Choose white if you want to feel open to new ideas, need space to think, seek clarity and peace.
Avoid white if you're unsure or insecure.

Choose cream as an undistracting backdrop to an intense lifestyle.
Avoid cream if you feel uninteresting or uninterested, lacking focus in your life.

Choose black if you're assured, successful, want to defend yourself.
Avoid black if you're low on self-confidence and feel anxious.

Choose red where you need to keep alert or if you are always full of energy.
Avoid red if you tire easily or suffer from claustrophobia.

Choose orange to create a cheerful and sociable atmosphere.
Avoid orange in bedrooms or if you're under stress.

Choose pink in warm shades for the bedroom, to blend caring and passion.
Avoid pink in cool pastels which blunt drive and energy.

Choose yellow as a revitaliser if you're depressed and sluggish.
Avoid yellow in bedrooms and studies, if you tend to be impulsive.

Choose green if you're introverted, or in a stressful job that involves handling people.
Avoid green if you're lethargic, empty of feeling or withdrawn.

Choose blue for relaxation and harmony; to calm a go-getting nature.
Avoid blue if you feel passive and unambitious – it can be *too* soothing.

SPECIAL EFFECTS

Painted decorative effects have been enjoying a big revival in popularity recently, and it's easy to see why. Sponging, rag-rolling, spattering and stencilling give rooms a smart 'designer' look, and add individuality in colours carefully chosen to blend with the furnishings.

The effects can be applied to a variety of surfaces, from walls and woodwork to ceramic tiling. Probably the simplest technique is sponging – creating delicate cloud effects by sponging colour on to a painted base with natural or synthetic sponges.

Above: Painstaking care was needed to create this beautiful marble finish with its fascinating veined surface.

For the soft mottled effect of rag-rolling, clean white rags are crumpled and literally rolled over the second coat as it is drying, and the interesting flecked look of spattering is best achieved by brushing contrasting paint on to the base coat through an open mesh 'grid'.

Stencilling offers plenty of scope for creative colour schemes – you can cut out your own designs from a sheet of acetate film, or buy pre-cut stencils from decorating shops.

All these techniques are simple to master, but you do need to practise them first to ensure consistent results. Experiment with different colours and combinations by using paint from small tester pots on a piece of hardboard.

Rag rolling adds a hint of texture and is an easy effect to achieve successfully.

The delicate effect used on the tongue-and-groove walls also suffuses the floor with a wash of soft pastel colour.

The exciting selection of wallcoverings available means that choosing the design is often the hardest part of the job. As well as the style of room, you will need to consider practicality. The essential advice is to take your time, both when choosing the paper and hanging it. The finished result will be well worth all the hours and effort involved.

WALLPAPER

Patterns and plains

Choosing a style

The tools you'll need

Preparing the surface

What type of paper?

Step-by-step hanging guide

Apart from the expense of changing your mind, wall-papering itself can be tricky, so you'll want to get your choice right first time. As well as thinking about the overall look you want, remember how the room will be used: when decorating a bedroom, for instance, you can afford to use paler and less practical colours and finishes than you would pick for a living room or hall.

Choosing a pattern

Patterned papers can be very pretty, but bear in mind how they will look in large expanses. Small, stylised floral patterns create a country cottage feel in any type of room, especially when combined with pine furniture. It's best to keep them for smaller rooms though, as they can look too busy if used over a large area of wall. You can break up the design by using a matching wallpaper border or dado rail.

Larger flowery designs featuring roses, ribbons and garlands, immediately conjure up thoughts of grand English country

Left: Papers which imitate marbled and stippled paint effects can look very convincing.

Right: A border banded in deep rose pink makes an eye-catching dividing line between elegant stripes and fresh florals.

Tools for the job

Using the right tools will make the job easier and help you achieve a better end result.

Plastic bucket for paste A taut string tied across the bucket between the ends of the handle is useful for wiping excess paste off the brush.

Paste Most pastes come as dry flakes or powders which are mixed with water. Use all-purpose paste for light- to medium-weight papers. For heavier embossed papers, use heavy-duty paste or ready-mixed paste. Vinyls and washable papers should be hung with a fungicidal paste which inhibits the growth of mould under the paper. If you are using ready-pasted paper, you will need a water trough for soaking.

Plumb bob and chalk For marking straight guidelines on the wall. Make one by tying a small weight, such as a pair of pliers, to a piece of string.

Pasting table These can be bought quite cheaply, and some versions have a useful built-in straight edge and measure. Otherwise, you can improvise by laying a sheet of chipboard over a table.

Decorating rule with integral spirit level For measuring walls and corners.

Steel tape measure For measuring lengths of paper.

Sponge For wiping excess paste off paper.

Handleless paper-hanging brush For smoothing the paper on to the wall.

Seam roller For getting good, flat seams.

Paste brush.

Scissors with long blades.

Step ladder.

Far right: The formal striped paper is softened by using a more diffuse pattern above the dado border.

houses. Many of the traditional florals available today are based on designs from the last century. However, as the patterns are often big, they can be overwhelming if used to cover a large area. Combine them with a matching plain paper and plain fabrics to pick out one of the colours from the design.

Stripes create a very classic look which never dates and works equally well with both contemporary and traditional furnishing. They help to lengthen walls visually, thus giving a room more height, but care should be taken when hanging them, as the slightest mistake will show. Another choice for a classic look is moire, which gives the impression of watered silk and looks especially good with traditional furnishings.

Papers that imitate painted effects such as sponging, ragging or marbling are available in a wide range of designs and colours. Halfway between plain and patterned, they are a good choice as a background to highly patterned fabrics. The random effect of the design also makes them fairly easy to hang.

Before you start

Preparation Remove old wall coverings by soaking with warm water and washing-up liquid before scraping off with a stripping knife. Make sure walls are clean, sound and dry. Fill holes or cracks with filler and sand smooth when dry. Recently plastered surfaces need to be 'sized' with a coat of diluted paste.

Getting ready Check that the pattern is the correct way up on all the rolls. If not, reverse wind the roll. Paper ceilings first. Start walls next to a window and paper away from the light source. Always make a vertical on each wall, using a plumb line or long spirit level, every time you turn a corner.

Cutting Measure the height of the wall and cut a corresponding length of paper, allowing 5 cm top and bottom for trimming. Cut the first length of boldly patterned papers so that there will be a complete motif at the top. Use your first cut length as a guide to matching the pattern on further pieces and mark a scale on the edge of your pasting table to help with measuring.

For easy pattern matching, lay three rolls of paper on top of one another, pattern side down. Use bulldog clips to hold them and allow the excess of each roll to sit on the floor at one end. Check the pattern matches on each piece and mark the tops with a pencil. Re-check length before cutting with a sharp trimming knife and straight edge.

check point

Guide to wallcoverings

Lining paper Only needed if the surface is poor or has been previously painted, or with a 'special' wall covering such as hessian or cork (see below).

Woodchip Paper with pieces of embedded wood to give a textured finish when painted. Good for disguising damaged walls.

Relief wallcoverings Have an embossed pattern to paint over. Good for disguising poor surfaces.

Ordinary wallpaper Printed, plain or patterned. Usually spongeable but rarely washable so unsuitable for heavy-wear areas.

Washable or vinyl-coated A printed paper with thin vinyl coating which can be cleaned with a cloth and soapy water. Quite hard-wearing. Good for kitchens and kids' rooms.

Paper-backed vinyl Plastic film on a paper backing sheet. May have embossed pattern. Can be cleaned with a mild abrasive. Ideal for kitchens and bathrooms.

Foamed vinyl Paper backing and a top surface of PVC. Usually imitates tiling. Also water-resistant, so a good alternative to ceramic tiles for kitchens and bathrooms.

'Special' wall coverings All papers with textile or 'natural' finishes, including silk, hessian, grasscloth and cork. Often very expensive. May require special hanging methods and adhesive.

HANGING PAPER STEP BY STEP

1 Mix your paste according to packet instructions. **Place your first cut length of paper face down on the pasting table. With the pasting brush, brush the paste along the entire length and work it out towards the edges. Try to ensure that the paper overlaps the table slightly to prevent paste getting on to the patterned side.**
2 Leave the pasted paper for a few minutes to absorb enough moisture for it to become supple. This also helps to avoid wrinkles and bubbles when the paper is hung. The time you need to leave it will depend on type of paper. Read instructions on label. Fold pasted surfaces together, bringing top and bottom to meet in the middle. For longer lengths fold like a concertina.

3 Check which is the top end of the length and carry the folded length over one arm to the wall.
4 Hold the top corners, open the top fold and stick the top half of the length on the wall. Then, allowing 5 cm (2 in) at the ceiling line for trimming, slide the paper exactly into position. Smooth down the middle of the paper with the paper-hanging brush, working out towards the edges to remove the wrinkles and air bubbles as you go.

5 Unfold the rest of the paper and continue to smooth down, leaving a similar trimming margin of 5 cm (2 in) at the bottom of the wall.
6 Run the back of your scissors along the angle of the ceiling and the skirting to mark where the paper has to be trimmed. Gently pull the paper away from the wall and trim off the excess. Wipe off excess paste from the ceiling and skirting with a damp sponge, and brush down the edges of the paper.

7 Position the next length of paper on the wall beside the first and slide it into position against the first piece so that the pattern matches at eye level. If wrinkles appear, there are still air pockets under the paper. Gently peel the paper back and brush it down again. Minor wrinkles will disappear on drying.
8 If necessary, gently use the seam roller to flatten the joins about 20 minutes after hanging. Don't roll embossed or relief papers.

9 Never hang a full width of paper round an inside corner; always hang

the paper in two parts. First measure the distance from the last piece you have hung to the corner. Do this at several points from skirting to ceiling to find the greatest distance.

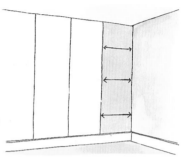

10 Cut a strip of paper 1 cm ($\frac{1}{2}$ in) wider than this distance, paste and hang it with the extra 1 cm ($\frac{1}{2}$ in) overlapping on to the next wall. Measure the width of the offcut from the corner and mark a vertical this distance from the corner on to the side wall. Paste the offcut, aligning the uncut edge with the vertical line so that the cut edge fits flush into the corner and covers the overlap. Treat external corners in the same way.

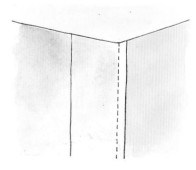

11 Before papering round a light switch or socket, turn off electricity at mains – don't forget you're using water. Smooth the length of paper very gently over the fitting. For square fittings, pierce the paper at the centre of the fitting and make four diagonal cuts from the centre to approximately 2.5 cm (1 in) beyond each corner.

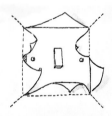

14 Papering a ceiling can be difficult for a beginner working alone. It is better to have a helper to support lengths of paper while you work. The basic method is the same as for papering a wall. You should paper across the room, working away from the window. Before you start, mark a straight guideline on the ceiling about 1 cm ($\frac{1}{2}$ in) less than one paper width away from the wall.

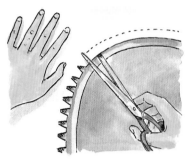

12 Press the paper round the edge of the fitting and lightly pencil round the outline. Trim away the excess, leaving 3 mm–4 mm ($\frac{1}{4}$ in) extra all round to brush behind the plate. Partially unscrew the plate and pull away from the wall. Brush the extra paper behind the plate and screw back in place. Never brush metallic or foil wall coverings behind the plate as they could conduct electricity. Instead, cut to fit around the switch.

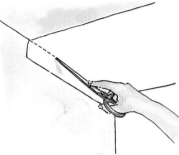

15 Cut a length of paper allowing 5 cm (2 in) overlap at each end. Paste and fold the paper as before. Position the paper against the guideline, supporting the spare folds with a roll of paper or similar object. Unfold the paper bit by bit and brush into position. Score and trim each end.

17 Remember to mark any existing screw holes (from shelves for example) as soon as you have hung the paper, while you can still see where they are. Mark them with matchsticks so you can locate them when the paper has dried.

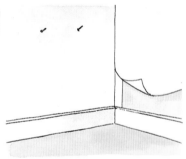

HANGING BORDERS

Draw a pencil line as a guide and cut a piece of border the full length of the wall. Paste the border and fold it concertina fashion. Then, using the line as a guide, unfold the border and brush it into place. Corners around a door or window should be mitred: overlap borders where they meet, and draw a diagonal line across the corner. Cut along the line through both layers, using a craft knife. Remove excess pieces.

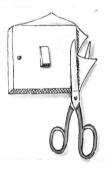

13 For round switches, make a series of star-shaped cuts in the paper, press down, mark and trim in the same way as for square fittings.

16 To paper an archway, paper the facing wall first, allowing an extra 2.5 cm (1 in) of paper around the inside of the arch. Cut V-shaped pieces out of this hem so that you are left with a saw-toothed effect. Turn in the teeth so that they lie flat on the inside of the arch. Then measure the width of the arch and cut two lengths of paper, one to run up each side so that they meet in the centre at the top.

For a durable and good-looking finish, it's hard to beat tiles. Use them on walls and worktops; round sinks, baths and showers; or as a surround for a fireplace or stove. Tiles are ideal anywhere you want a surface that wipes clean and stands up well to everyday wear and tear. And hanging them is straightforward, once you've acquired the knack.

TILES

Surface preparation
Estimating quantities
Different types explained
Tiling tools
Fixing tiles step-by-step
Cutting awkward shapes

Ceramic tiles can create unique decorative effects, providing a stylish and practical finish for kitchens, bathrooms and fireplaces. The choice of designs is huge, from the charming, rustic quality of imported tiles, to the detailed decoration on reproduction Victorian and Edwardian styles.

Plain tiles, in a standard range of colours, are available quite cheaply, but you may have to pay substantially more for highly decorated or hand-painted versions. Before you buy, check that the tiles are appropriate for the place where you intend to use them. Tiles which are going to get a thorough dowsing in the shower or bathroom should have a tough glaze which can stand up to hot water, while those intended to be used near a fireplace or hob should be heat-resistant to avoid cracking.

Before you start ...

As with all decorating jobs, it pays off to prepare the surfaces properly before you start tiling. The walls must be clean and dry. Any damp patches should be treated, and fresh plaster should be given time to dry thoroughly. Any crumbling patches of plaster should be repaired.

A twisted rope border adds distinction to inexpensive plain white tiles. Aqua towels and bath mat reinforce the colour theme.

check point

Guide to tiles

Universal tiles
Have angled edges which
space tiles for grouting
automatically. Some come
with glazed edges, so that
they can be used around the
sides of the tiled area.

Decorative border tiles
Designed to form a
decorative edging, these are
long and narrow. Usually
they co-ordinate with a
range of square tiles.

Standard field tiles
Need spacer lugs to create
room for grout.

Corner tiles
Have two rounded edges to
provide a neat finish on
corners.

Insert tiles
Incorporate accessories such
as soap dishes, towel rails
and toilet roll holders and
can be positioned as part of a
run of standard tiles.

Mosaic tiles
Are small ceramic or glass
tiles, usually mounted on
paper or webbed backing
with space for grouting.

Ceramic trims
Used to finish edges in
kitchens and bathrooms.

Don't be tempted to hang tiles on to wallpaper. The weight will
pull the paper off, so strip the paper before beginning. You can tile
on to paint if the surface is good. Rub down any flaky patches and
roughen the surface all over with sandpaper. You can also tile
straight on to old tiles. Clean them first, and roughen the surface
with a scriber. However, if you do lay new tiles over existing ones,
adjust the starting level so that grout points don't coincide.

The walls must be flat. If the walls have lumps and bumps, it
may be easier to cover the entire surface with chipboard or
plywood, sealed with a coat of diluted PVA.

Warm terracotta-coloured wall tiles offset the coolness of the cream flooring and bath suite.

Getting started

To estimate the number of tiles you will need to buy, multiply the height and width of the area(s) to be covered to find the number of square metres or yards of tiles you require. Allow an extra five per cent for breakages and mistakes.

When shopping, try to buy packs stamped with the same batch number. If this is impossible, mix the tiles from different batches before you start in order to avoid noticeable colour variations.

A mixture of plain and patterned tiles can look very effective, and is cheaper than using all patterned tiles. Plot the design on graph paper before you begin.

Aim for a symmetrical finish on plain walls, and tile outwards from the middle, making the two sides identical. If there is a window on the wall, use the centre of the window as your starting point, and if there are two windows, start from a vertical line drawn midway between them.

A scattering of patterned tiles enlivens an otherwise plain green and white colour scheme, and subtly emphasises the intriguing shapes of chimney breast and alcove.

check point

Tools for the job

Tile adhesive Use a standard adhesive, or a waterproof one for bathrooms, showers and sink splashbacks. Some adhesives can also be used as grout.

Adhesive spreader

Grout This is a plaster paste used to fill the gaps between tiles once they have been hung. It is available in white and assorted colours.

Sponge or cloth Use damp for applying grout.

Tile cutter For cutting tiles to fit around awkward shapes.

Tile spacers Little pieces of plastic which you insert between tiles as they are hung to make sure they are evenly spaced.

Battening Use this to position your first row of tiles accurately.

Spirit level

Tape measure

Tile nippers or pincers For nibbling out difficult shapes when cutting tiles.

FIXING TILES STEP BY STEP

1 Nail a straight wooden batten along the wall, one tile depth above the skirting board. Don't assume that the skirting board is straight: use a spirit level. (You may need masonry nails if hammering into an existing layer of tiles.)

2 Spread adhesive over the wall above the batten covering 1 sq m (10 sq ft) at a time using a notched spreader. This will make a wavy pattern in the glue, which helps the tiles to stick.

3 Start fixing the tiles to the wall. Give each a slight twist as you press in place to ensure a good contact. The bottom edge of the tile should rest against the top of the batten.

4 Fix tiles along the length of the batten, inserting plastic spacers between them as you go. These ensure that the grout joints are of a uniform thickness across the wall.

5 Bed spacers down below the level of the tiles so that the grout will cover them – some tiles now have angled edges which do away with the need for spacers.

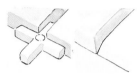

6 For the moment, leave gaps at the ends where you will need to cut tiles. Complete two or three rows of whole tiles first, to get a good feel for the job.

7 The traditional way of cutting tiles takes a bit of practice. First, measure the gap to be filled with a steel tape and transfer the measurements on to the glazed side of the tile with a marker pen. Score along

the pen line with a scriber, going just deep enough to cut the glaze. Position the tile face up over a couple of matchsticks lined up with the score and press gently. It should snap quite cleanly and easily.

8 It's far easier to use a modern tile jig/cutter. This will transfer the shape of the gap accurately on to the tile, and guide your hand when you're wielding the scriber.
9 Smooth the cut edge with a file or abrasive paper before fixing the tile in place. File in one direction only – away from the glaze.
10 To fit around washbasins etc, you will need to make a template. Cut the shape of the curve into a piece of card and transfer this outline on to a tile. Cut away the unwanted section of the tile with nibblers or pincers, a little bit at a time. Smooth the edges with a file.

11 To cut a hole from the centre of a tile to fit it around a pipe, slice the tile in half and cut two matching half circles.
12 When tiling around a window recess, try to position the cut tiles next to the window itself.

13 For a really neat finish, use an edging strip at the front of the recess where it meets the wall.
14 You will probably need to cut a tile to an L-shape to fit the wall around each corner of the recess. To do this, cut a line from the edge of the tile to the centre with a tile saw. Then score a line at right angles to the cut and snap off the unwanted piece.
15 Leave the tiles for 24 hours before you begin filling the gaps between them with grout. Press the grout into place with a small sponge.
16 While the grout is still wet, wipe off any excess from the face of the tiles with a clean sponge.
17 Smooth down the surface of the grout with the blunt end of a pencil. Any unwanted grout that hardens on the surface of the tiles themselves should be carefully scratched off with a razor blade.
18 If you need to drill a hole through the tile to attach a

mirror or bathroom cabinet to the wall, cover the spot first with a piece of masking tape. This will prevent the drill from slipping and scratching the tiled surface. You can use a masonry drill bit for the job, although special tile drill bits are also available.

Choosing the right flooring for each room means balancing appearance and toughness against your budget. Carpet need not be extravagantly expensive if you choose carefully; but there are other flooring options which can be softened with inexpensive rugs if you prefer. Don't be bewildered by the huge choice of weaves and fibres, tiles and vinyls in the shops, but wise up on the flooring facts before you make a decision.

CARPETS
and floorings

Wool and synthetics

Weight and wearability

Woven or tufted?

Guide to buying rugs

Wooden floors • Vinyls • Tiles

How to lay flooring

A carpet is probably the biggest and most important furnishing investment you'll make in any room, but don't be seduced into choosing one just because it is the perfect colour or pattern to fit in with your decorating scheme. The first priority should always be quality.

Cheap, lightweight carpet laid in heavy-wear areas will last for only a short period. A better quality always pays off in terms of wear, comfort and appearance.

Fibre facts

Should you choose wool or man-made? Wool is well tried and tested. Its natural crimp enables fibres to resist pressure from heavy furniture and it retains its appearance for a long time. However, many man-made fibres have been 'engineered' to look and feel more like wool. Their good qualities are improved resilience and anti-static, and some come with Scotchguard treatments to block staining. You could of course opt for the best of both worlds, and go for a mixture of fibres. A blend of 80/20 wool/nylon combines the resilience of the natural wool with the strength and toughness of man-made nylon. As the percentage of wool decreases so does the quality and the price.

Go for a carpet with mottled effect in heavy traffic areas such as sitting rooms, where a plain finish would show every mark.

Quality underfoot

There is no one grading scheme common to all carpets. You need to study the individual label, though most larger stores detail the uses very clearly. The pile weights per sq yd (usually shown on the label or display material) are a good guide to use. For example, the minimum quality for a living room carpet used by two adults should be about 31 oz per sq yd. For a family of four, where the wear will be greater, it should be 33 oz or 34 oz per sq yd.

Dark apricot carpet makes this sitting room feel immediately warm and welcoming. The small, regular pattern is practical as well as attractive.

For hall, landings and particularly stairs, the minimum pile weight for family use should be 35 oz per sq yd. For bedrooms and lesser-used areas like studies, lighter weights, under 28 oz are usually suitable.

Remember that the biggest threats to carpets are shoes and animals. Trainer shoes may seem soft underfoot, but they're bad news for carpets, particularly velvet pile, as are stiletto heels.

Plain or patterned?

Plains are a good choice in small houses or flats because they give a feeling of space. They are particularly suitable in households where they won't be subjected to a lot of heavy wear, or where there are no small children. Pale colours look marvellous, but avoid them unless you are prepared to be on constant guard against stains. A plain velvet carpet creates a feeling of luxury. Be sure the pile is fairly dense – sink your fingers into it. 'Shading' can be a problem when the pile is flattened by use, but it can usually be removed by vacuuming.

Patterned carpets are good for disguising footmarks and signs of wear and tear, and they need not be garish. There's a good choice of elegant traditional and small modern designs. Some manufacturers also produce designs to match their soft furnishing fabrics. A good practical compromise is a Berber carpet, where two neutral shades are used to make a textured finish that is very effective at disguising dirt.

Luscious, rich designs work best in large rooms where they can be seen to their full effect. Keep other fabrics fairly plain, to avoid swamping the room with pattern.

Woven or tufted?

Woven carpets – Axminsters and Wiltons – are made by craftsmen who have developed their expertise over hundreds of years. Multi-coloured patterned carpets are usually woven on *Axminster* looms, which give clear design definition. Up to 35 colours may be used at a time, and backing and pile are woven simultaneously. *Wilton* carpets are usually in plain colours, though up to five can be used to make a pattern. They tend to be of higher quality and therefore more expensive than Axminsters. The pile is denser because surplus yarn is buried between the base of the pile and the backing.

Tufted carpets are much more economical to produce. The pile is needled into a pre-woven backing. There is a good choice of small patterns and mottled effects as well as plains, and many are made in wool.

Rugs

Loose-laid rugs are the easiest way of effecting a magic transformation to a plain carpeted, wood or parquet floor. They add instant colour, create an attractive focal point or highlight existing features such as a fireplace and – best of all – they can be moved and changed to match your furnishings or echo the season.

What to look for

● A good quality rug should be dense and firm.
● Most pile rugs are 100 per cent pure new wool: the Woolmark symbol is an assurance that it meets specified standards. Cotton, jute and linen are also used.
● Be sure the rug is well finished, with no ragged edges.

Guide to rugs

Bokhara Fine cut-pile rug from Pakistan, hand-washed to give a very high sheen.
Dhurrie Flat-woven wool or cotton rug, synonymous with India.
Kelim Wool carpet from Turkey, flat-woven in geometric designs, often used as a wall hanging.
Numdah Embroidered rug from Kashmir, made from wool and cotton felted together under water pressure.
Rag rug Flat-woven cotton rug originating in Sweden. Do not use on pale carpets, as dye may stain.

OTHER FLOORING

Floors come in for a lot of wear and tear, especially in areas of heavy traffic. In places where carpet would be inappropriate, there is a good choice of durable alternatives. Before you make up your mind, take a careful look at your budget and always buy the best quality you can afford.

The surface on which you plan to lay the new flooring should be damp-proof and in good condition. Timber floors must be strong enough to support a heavy surface, such as quarry tiles, so check the condition of joists and boards before starting, particularly in older properties. Remove any protruding nails and smooth down rough patches and splinters. Concrete floors should be even, with no lumps and bumps which might show through a flooring like sheet vinyl.

Wooden floors

Although not suitable for kitchens and bathrooms, these are very hard-wearing as long as the surface is well sealed. They look attractive, and can be softened with rugs or matting as long as these are non-slip. This creates a warmer effect and helps to deaden the sound of footsteps. If your floorboards are in reasonable condition, you can sand and seal them (see page 96). Make sure that any gaps between boards are filled, to avoid draughts. Once the boards are sealed they should stand up fairly well to spills, but wipe up liquids quickly, before they have a chance to stain.

You can also lay a new wooden floor, using hardwood blocks or strips. Again, these finishes are unsuitable for kitchens or bathrooms, and some of them should be laid by a professional.

Cleaning Sweep or vacuum the surface regularly, polish as needed (but don't polish under rugs unless they are non-slip).

Large quarry flags give this dining area a rustic feeling which is in keeping with the view of woods outside. A rug adds colour to a simple room which is otherwise soothingly neutral.

Cork

Cork tiles are easy to lay and, as they are slip-resistant when wet, are suitable for kitchens and bathrooms. They usually come in shades of gold or brown and are warm to look at and soft to stand on. Cork must be sealed if it is likely to come into contact with water, otherwise it will absorb liquid and may start to rise from the floor. Square or rectangular tiles are available in different thicknesses. Cork dents easily, so should not be used where heavy furniture will stand on it.

Cleaning Use a damp mop. Polish sealed cork occasionally with a suitable wax.

Vinyl

Cushioned vinyl, which has a layer of tiny air bubbles between the top surface and the backing to make it soft to walk on, usually comes in sheets. It feels warm to the touch and deadens sound effectively. Thinner, non-cushioned, vinyls come in sheet or tile form. They are less expensive than the cushioned type, but may not wear as well, are less warm underfoot and can be slippery when wet.

Vinyl is very suitable for places where it might get wet. Numerous designs are available, from plain colours to cork or tiled effects. Don't choose an extra-soft cushioned vinyl for a kitchen or utility room, where it might be damaged by sharp objects or heavy equipment.

Cleaning Wipe over regularly with a damp mop or cloth, and use an acrylic polish to give the surface more protection.

Quarry tiles

The earthy shades of brown and terracotta look lovely in a country-style kitchen. Quarry tiles wear well, but are noisy, as well as being hard and cold to stand on for any length of time. Because they are so tough, anything dropped on to them will break. They can be slippery when wet and tend to absorb stains. When buying, check that the tiles are the correct thickness for laying on a floor. Wall tiles are thinner and lighter.

Cleaning Easily done with water and floor cleaner. The colour can be kept bright by applying a special polish when the floor shows signs of fading.

Blue and white mosaic effect tiles used in the kitchen give way to a plain blue carpet for the dining area.

Far right: Closely woven rush flooring is hard-wearing enough to use in a hall. This material would be too rigid to lay easily on the stairs, however, so they are carpeted.

Rush or sisal floorings

Natural materials such as coir, rush matting or sisal, are cheap and wear well. These floorings are easy to cut to shape and lay. Some versions come with a vinyl or latex backing to keep down dust levels. Colours are usually beiges, browns or golds, although the fibres can be dyed in other colours, or have different fibres mixed in. Some natural fibres are rather coarse and may be unkind to bare feet. For this reason, they are not always suitable for use in children's rooms.

Cleaning Vacuum regularly. Cut off any loose or jagged ends that appear. Unbacked floorings allow a lot of dust through, and the flooring will have to be rolled back from time to time so that the surface beneath can be cleaned.

Laying flooring

● Although a person competent at DIY can lay a vinyl or cork floor, if in any doubt it is a job best left to experts. Awkwardly shaped rooms, with bays, hearths and alcoves are particularly tricky, as the flooring has to be cut precisely to fit and expensive mistakes can be made.

● Tiles are easier to lay than sheet flooring. Their small size makes them simple to handle, and mistakes are less wasteful.

● The sub-floor should be clean, dry and smooth. Sweep thoroughly, or wash if appropriate, and allow to dry completely.

● If the flooring is being laid on to a concrete floor, check that there is a damp proof membrane.

● Leave cork tiles or vinyl in the room where they are to be laid for 24 hours before laying, to give them time to acclimatise to the room temperature.

● Do not lay vinyl on timber floors treated with preservative, brown asphalt tiles or asphalt floors, cork tiles or linoleum. Ask your supplier for details of a barrier material to lay between the existing floor and the vinyl.

A well-dressed window transforms the whole room by providing an injection of colour and interest. The possibilities range from neat roller blinds to grand floor-length curtains decked with frills and swags. You can even mix several effects at the same window to get the result you're after. Here's how to select the style that suits the room.

WINDOW
treatments

Creating clever effects
Choosing the right style
Ready-mades • Sewing your own
Colours and patterns
All kinds of blinds

Stylish window decoration has become an important focal point in any furnishing scheme. You can make or buy a huge range of window dressing: 'dress' curtains, which stay fixed to frame the window, while you open and close a teaming blind for privacy; elaborate swags and tails; festoon blinds and pleated valances; and to complete the look, tie-backs to match cushions, a headboard or lampshades.

Dramatic effects

Because window dressings frame the main light source in a room people's eyes automatically focus on them. Instead of completely re-decorating a room, you can dramatically alter its appearance by simply giving the window a new treatment.

You can inject life into a small and rather dull room by using curtains or a blind in a sunny shade or soft pastel colour, and introduce a feeling of warmth and grandeur to a large room that may have a cold atmosphere by dressing the window in rich and sumptuous dark-toned fabrics.

It's easy to create a country cottage look by using small-scale sprigged floral patterns, and in the same way you can bring a romantic atmosphere to a bedroom with a ruched, frilled Austrian blind, or emphasise the sleek lines of modern furniture in a lounge or dining room by using curtains in a distinctive abstract print to frame neat slim- or vertical-slatted blinds.

A long, frilled curtain swept smoothly across a corner window lets in sufficient light and adds colour to the room.

In the shops

As the interest in window treatments has grown, so has the choice of ideas in the shops. There is now an enormous selection on offer, many designed to be bought as ready-made sets in teaming colours and patterns. If you're sewing your own window dressings, you will find a wide selection of heading tapes, tracks and decorative poles for achieving a professional look – and there are plenty of clever short cuts to help you tackle the more elaborate effects. The latest track systems also enable two or more window treatments to be hung neatly together.

Selecting the style

How do you set about choosing a style that will suit *your* room, from what can seem a bewildering array of different window dressings and accessories? There are a number of practical steps that will help you make up your mind.

First, consider the sort of effect you want to create, bearing in mind the style of your existing furnishings and the way the room is used. Do you, for example, want the curtains or blinds to bring some drama to a dining room, to soften the atmosphere of a clinical bathroom, or to make your hall more welcoming?

Could you improve the proportions of a room by extending the curtain track to make the window appear wider, or give it an illusion of being taller, by positioning the track high above the top of the frame, and adding a deep valance?

The next step is to link your choice of colour and pattern with the kind of effects you are trying to create. The basic scheming rules will help here: for a warmer look, go for rich red, cheerful yellow or orange tones; for a cooler, refreshing aspect, choose from the other end of the spectrum and use blue, grey or white; and if you're after a comfortable country look, select shades of browns, greens and naturals.

An unfussy treatment gives maximum impact to the view outside. Densely gathered curtains hang from a simple pole and can be pulled right back to reveal the entire window, or left half-drawn to create a frame.

Curtains which match the bed linen can be used to conceal the windowseat, or left permanently tied back. The window itself is covered with a gauzy festoon blind.

check point

Making curtains and blinds

- Many manufacturers produce helpful booklets.
- Large designs look marvellous on full-length curtains, but remember that you will have to buy extra fabric to match the pattern.
- Don't be mean with fabric, otherwise curtains will look skimpy.
- Linings help curtains to hang well, and also keep out light and draughts. In a very cold room you could use a thermal interlining as well.
- Let the curtains hang for a week or more before hemming, so that the fabric can drop.
- Roller blinds are the simplest to make, although tapes and kits are available for making other types.
- Choose a firm cotton fabric with a close weave. Anything too light or heavy will not roll up smoothly.
- Be careful when cutting to get edges perfectly straight.
- Use a stiffener spray to give the fabric a wipeable finish. Don't cut the blind to its final size until after spraying, as the fabric may shrink slightly.

A simple blind is the best solution for a long, narrow window. A lace curtain gives privacy.

Choose the pattern and fabric to echo the room style and give it a total look. If your decor is traditional, for example, there's a wealth of floral designs in different scales to choose from, as well as Regency stripes, luxurious velvets, and ornate lace sheers.

Then you need to investigate which of the many different styles of curtains, headings, valances and blinds would best achieve the effect you want, and decide whether you can make the window dressings yourself, buy ready-mades, or have them made to order.

At this stage, you will find it's very helpful to visit your nearest department store or soft furnishings specialist to chat to one of their experts, and to take home a selection of brochures and price lists showing different manufacturers' ideas.

Opting for blinds

One disadvantage of putting curtains at your windows is that they use a great deal of fabric, and are inevitably expensive. Blinds are a cheaper alternative which can look very effective. Remember, however, that blinds cannot disguise an ugly window, and are not as efficient as curtains at excluding draughts.

Roller blinds are the simplest type. If you want them to cover a large window, use two or more blinds, as one enormous one may not hang well. Roller blinds can be given a softer look with a scalloped or frilled trim along the lower edge.

Roman blinds look much like roller blinds when they are let down, but when opened fold upwards into deep pleats, which make a loose pelmet effect at the top of the window. They look good in fairly formal rooms.

Austrian or festoon blinds are ruched to hang in rich swags. They can be trimmed with braid or fringing for a more opulent look. Choose them for a long, fairly narrow window, rather than a wide one.

Venetian blinds have slats which can be opened or closed to control the amount of light entering the room. They are available in a wide range of colours and with slats of various widths, hung horizontally or vertically. They can be expensive, and tend to give a stark, architectural look.

Paper and wooden blinds are fairly inexpensive. Pleated paper blinds are the cheapest, come in a range of colours and are very practical. Blinds made of cane or thin slats of wood let the light filter through gently and are effective at a very sunny window.

THREE

DOING IT YOURSELF

There's nothing more satisfying than standing back to admire a DIY job well done. Lots of basic tasks are very straightforward, and many more complicated projects can be easily tackled by an amateur. And of course, any work you do yourself will save you money. Just allow lots of time, use the right tools, and follow these simple step-by-step guides.

CHANGING A TAP WASHER

There are three basic types of tap that need new washers when they start to drip: traditional cross-top (capstan-head) taps; chunky shroud-headed taps and supataps. If a tap with ceramic discs leaks, it's usually because a piece of grit has got between the discs and the problem should be dealt with by a professional.

CHOOSING A WASHER

Basin and sink taps have 12 mm ($\frac{1}{2}$ in) washers; bath taps have 19 mm ($\frac{3}{4}$ in) washers. There are hard rubber or leather washers for hot taps, soft ones for cold taps or plastic for either. Rubber washers can be cut to fit with a craft knife.

TOOLS AND MATERIALS

You will need an adjustable spanner, washers (or 'jumpers' for supataps), available from plumbers' suppliers.

GENERAL TAP MAINTENANCE

All taps should be washed regularly to avoid corrosion. Polish with a soft cloth (do not use abrasives).

Always match replacement washers to the size of the existing ones and remove all pieces of the old one.

Encourage children to turn off taps firmly: a dripping tap in a hard-water area will stain the sink. To remove persistent stains, rub with half a fresh lemon.

If you are fitting new taps, bear in mind the people who will be using them: children and the elderly can have difficulty in handling some designs.

CROSS-TOP TAP

1 Turn off the water supply at the stopcock and turn on the tap to let the water drain out.
2 Unscrew the top part of the tap (the shroud). If it sticks, pour over boiling water. If it still sticks, bang it with a spanner wrapped in a cloth.

3 Unscrew the main nut holding the main body of the tap and lift it clear.

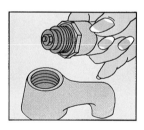

4 Unscrew the nut holding the washer.

5 Remove the washer and replace it with the new one.

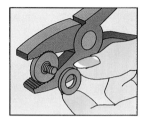

6 Screw all the parts of the tap together as before.

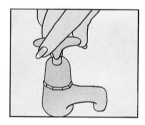

7 Turn on the water at the stopcock.

Cross-section of cross-top tap.

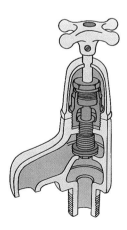

SHROUD-HEADED TAP

Moulded acrylic tap tops may be fixed with a main screw hidden under the H or C disc, which will have to be prised off. Or they may simply pull off with a sharp tug. From then on, work as for cross-top taps.

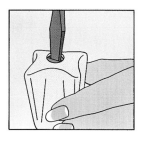

SUPATAPS

These are not often used now. If your house has them, you do not have to turn the water off to change the washer, or 'jumper'.

1 Loosen the top nut with a spanner.

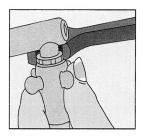

2 Turn the tap on and on and on until the handle comes off. At this stage the valve will automatically stop the flow of water to the tap.

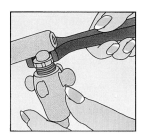

3 Gently press the knob on the spout onto a worktop to release the nozzle and jumper.

4 Turn the nozzle upside down and the jumper will fall out. Remove it with a screwdriver, clean the nozzle with a nailbrush and fit a new jumper.

5 Screw all the parts together as before.

PIPES, TANKS AND RADIATORS

LAGGING PIPES

Tools and materials
Scissors, sharp knife, felt strip or plastic foam, string, waterproof adhesive tape. Flexible foam plastic comes in sizes to fit any pipe between 6 mm ($\frac{1}{4}$ in) and 75 mm (3 in) diameter. Always use the correct size for the pipe.

Felt lagging
1 Wind round three times at tank end and bind with string.
2 Wrap strip diagonally, overlapping edges.

3 Bind each new strip of felt with string where it overlaps the previous one.

4 Wrap lagging generously round neck of valves, stopcocks etc.
5 Lag overflow pipes, concentrating on area next to outside wall.

Foam lagging
1 Wrap as for felt, making sure edges are close together.
2 Fix with adhesive tape round tank end.

3 At bends, push and tape edges together.
4 To seal joints, overlap pieces of foam and tape together.

LAGGING TANKS

Cold-water tanks
● Buy glass-fibre blanket material bonded with paper on one side for easier handling.
1 Cut to fit (if the tank is very large, you may have to use two overlapping pieces).
2 Secure with string and/or adhesive tape. Tape may help to hold blanket in place while you adjust it.
3 Start at base and overlap ends by 75 mm (3 in).

4 Cut slots where pipes enter tank and tuck the cut edges under the pipes.
5 Cut out a piece of material to overlap lid by about 150 mm (6 in). Do not tie.

Hot-water cylinders
The cheapest lagging is an old duvet, but a ready-made jacket (available from builders' merchants) is neater.

CLEARING RADIATOR AIR LOCKS

If a radiator is not heating up properly, air has probably become trapped somewhere. Bleed the system while the water is warm by opening the vent valve until water runs out freely.
● Most radiators have a square-ended hollow key (obtainable from hardware shops) to open the vent valve.
1 Insert key and turn anti-clockwise.
2 Hold a jar under the valve to collect water.
3 Tighten valve as soon as air stops escaping and water flows freely.
4 If necessary repeat process.

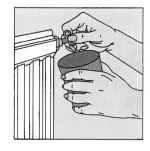

WASTE-PIPES AND DRAINAGE

MAINTAINING INDOOR WASTE-PIPES

Most kitchen sink blockages are caused by grease, hair and kitchen debris. These build up gradually in traps and waste-pipes, causing obstructions, sluggish water drainage and unpleasant smells.

● To maintain indoor waste-pipes, avoid pouring fat or cooking oil down the kitchen sink drain and use a sink tidy for scraps. Install drain-hole strainers on bathroom plug-holes to stop hair and soap scum clogging waste-pipes.

CLEANING WASTE-PIPES AND SHIFTING MINOR BLOCKAGES

● Although caustic soda (in jelly or crystal form) is often recommended for dissolving debris, this is a strong chemical cleaning agent which can damage textiles, paintwork and tiles and should not come into contact with the skin or eyes. You should always use caustic soda with care – wear rubber gloves and follow the manufacturer's instructions to the letter.

● A gentler (and greener) alternative for minor blockages and regular cleaning is to use washing soda crystals. Empty about a quarter of a standard 1 kg packet of washing crystals around the plug-hole and then pour on a kettle-full of very hot water. (Do not let the crystals come into contact with aluminium.)

USING A PLUNGER

If the water fails to drain from one sink, basin or bath in the house, while all the others are working normally, the obstruction must be in its own branch pipe. Try forcing the blockage out of the pipe by using a sink plunger – they're available from hardware and DIY stores:

1 To prevent air escaping through the overflow, stop it up with a wet cloth.

2 Make sure that there's enough water in the sink to cover the plunger's rubber cup. (If the sink's badly blocked, it will be full of water anyway.)

3 Hold the wet cloth in the overflow with one hand while you pump the handle of the plunger up and down.

4 If the water in the sink doesn't drain away immediately, the blockage may simply have been pushed a little further along the pipe, so try using the plunger again. If you don't have a plunger, try improvising by using a plastic bag, tied around the head of a mop or round a sponge tied to a stick.

CLEARING THE WASTE-PIPE TRAP

If the sink is still blocked, you may need to clear the trap. This is situated under the sink and it's common for debris to collect at the lowest point of the pipe's bend.

1 Place a bucket under the sink (or a tray if you're unblocking a bath pipe) to catch any water and debris that may be released.

2 Put the plug in.

3 Use a spanner or wrench to release the 'cleaning eye' or access cap on the U of the trap.

4 If your trap is bottle- rather than U-shaped, unscrew the access cap by hand.

(If there is no way that you can gain access to this part of the trap, unscrew the connecting nuts, remove the whole trap and then rinse it out.)

5 The contents of the trap (including the debris that is causing the blockage) should now drain into your bucket or tray.

MAJOR BLOCKAGES

Any major blockages involving exterior drains are often best left to the professionals.

● If your house is individually drained, the whole system is your responsibility until it joins the main sewer.

● If your exterior drain is linked to other homes, contact your environmental health officer to find out whether you are responsible for maintaining the drains.

Local councils should cleanse drains constructed before 1937, but this service isn't always free.

Communal drainage systems constructed after 1937 are the responsibility of all the householders concerned (so you and your neighbours will have to share the cost of repairs up to the sewer, no matter where the fault occurs).

FITTING A NEW WINDOW PANE

TOOLS AND MATERIALS

Cardboard, screwdriver, primer, putty, linseed oil, hammer, panel pins, meths or white spirit.

Note: Tape up the glass or remove it and cover the hole with polythene. Shattered glass should be broken into small pieces and wrapped and taped in thick layers of newspaper before being put in the dustbin.

1 Measure the rebate accurately to the nearest millimetre. The new piece should be 3 mm ($\frac{1}{8}$ in) less than your measurements. If the window is very out of true, make a template and take it with you to the glass merchants.

2 Put on a pair of old gloves and pull out the broken glass.

If the pane is held in with putty, cut it out with a screwdriver; if with glazing sprigs, discard them; if with wooden beading, carefully prise it up at the centre of one of the longest sides first, then at the ends. In metal windows, mark the position of the metal clips and use them again. Brush out all debris and paint the frame with primer.

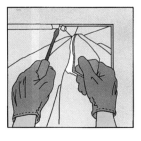

3 Knead a ball of putty until it is pliable. (Add more linseed oil if it is hard to mould.) Hold the putty in your hand and squeeze it out between thumb and forefinger to make a continuous ribbon round the rebate. (A little linseed oil smeared on before the putty will prevent wet getting in and rotting the frame.) You can use self-adhesive 'bedding tape' instead of putty: this is easier but more expensive.

4 Push the new pane in place against the putty, bottom first. Support it on matchsticks to give correct clearance all round. Press at the edges, NOT the centre. Gently hammer the sprigs or clips in place (running the hammer along the glass) at 30 cm (1 ft) intervals. Add another layer of putty to the outside of the glass, using a putty knife to get an angle of about 45°, which will allow water to run off.

● For beading, use less putty and fix with panel pins. Prime new beading first.

5 Remove putty smears with meths or white spirit and leave for a week or two (but not longer) before painting.

6 When painting, seal the edges by overlapping the paint on to the glass, or the putty will dry out and crack.

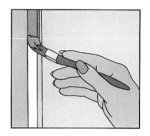

DRAUGHTPROOFING

ING IT YOURSELF

If you added up all the gaps between doors and windows and their frames, the hole would measure 1.2 sq m (12.9 sq ft) in the average house – plenty of room for heat to escape through! Draught-proofing is cheap, quick and easy and you will begin saving on fuel bills immediately.

WINDOWS AND DOORS

Sticky tape: Some windows can be kept closed all winter. Masking tape across the gaps will keep out draughts but it is not always easy to remove in spring, so don't use it unless you intend to redecorate then.
Foam strip: Adhesive foam strip can be fixed to the frame. This retracts when the window is closed, sealing gaps. It sticks to metal and wood and is invisible when windows are closed. It will not fill large gaps. Replace every two years.
● The frame should be dry and clean before applying.

Other types of interior draught excluder include **plastic strip** (a flexible tube which is squashed when the door closes to seal the gap), **V-shaped strips** and strips with **sprung**, **hinged flaps** in bronze, copper or plastic.

● Metal strips have a long life; plastic is cheaper and more flexible (good for crooked houses) but lasts only about three years.
● Read instructions and fix with care.

EXTERNAL DOORS

Easiest and cheapest is a plain strip of wood or plastic with an edge of bristles or rubber which brushes against the floor (below). For badly fitting doors, use an aluminium strip holding a plastic tube which compresses to form a seal.

FIREPLACES

Block off completely if not in use. Fix chipboard, plywood or cardboard cut to exact size over gap.

SKIRTINGS AND FLOORS

● Fill gaps between boards with papier mâché, bad gaps with slivers of wood fixed with wood glue.
● Carpet will help to eliminate any draughts.
● Nail strips of quadrant moulding where the skirting meets the floor and paint to match the skirting.

LETTERBOXES

Fix a close-fitting flap to the inner side so the flap swings inwards only, or fix a large box that covers the opening to inside of door to hold letters.

CAT FLAPS

Choose one that closes tightly to eliminate draughts – you can now get lockable flaps.

91

PUTTING UP SHELVES

Note: To make sure that your shelf will be secure, check that the wall is sound and dry. The thicker the shelves, the more weight they will hold. The distance needed between the supports to prevent shelves from bowing depends on what they will be used for and what they're made of:

15 mm ($\frac{5}{8}$ in) hardwood: support every 50 cm (20 in).
18 mm ($\frac{3}{4}$ in) plywood: support every 80 cm (30 in).
12 mm ($\frac{1}{2}$ in) blockboard: support every 45 cm (18 in).
18 mm ($\frac{3}{4}$ in) MDF: support every 70 cm (27 in).
18 mm ($\frac{3}{4}$ in) melamine-covered chipboard: support every 50 cm (20 in).
10 mm ($\frac{3}{8}$ in) glass: support every 70 cm (27 in).

TOOLS

Drill, wall plugs, bradawl, plumb-line, spirit level.

SUPPORT SYSTEMS

Various methods of supporting shelves are available:
● Individual non-adjustable metal brackets, ranging from the very cheap and basic to ornamental wrought iron.
● Individual non-adjustable horizontal strips of metal or wood. The shelf either rests on them or slots into them.

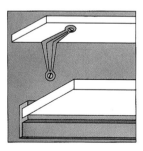

● Metal uprights with adjustable brackets available in different lengths to hold different depths of shelf.
● Wooden adjustable shelving with dowel supports: suitable for display shelving because the supports are almost invisible.

UPRIGHTS AND BRACKETS

This job is far easier if you get a friend to help.
1 Work out where you want your two uprights, and fix the top of one loosely to the wall.
2 Hang a plumb-line (or stone tied to a piece of string) from the top to align the upright vertically and mark the point for the bottom screw.

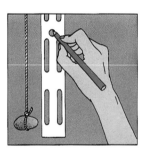

3 Clip a pair of brackets into position at equal levels on the two uprights. Ask a friend to hold the second upright against the wall while you lay a shelf across the brackets and check that the horizontal is true with a spirit level.

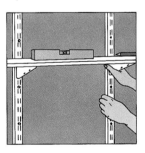

4 Now mark the final screw positions.

Notes
● Use a spirit level to check that individual brackets are correctly positioned.
● Screw brackets to shelves to prevent them from overbalancing.
● To finish long shelves, add end boards to hold books etc in place.
● To make a shelf look more substantial, fix a strip of hardwood along the front to form a lip.

WALL FIXINGS

Note: Make sure you don't drill into wires or pipes inside the wall. If fixing shelves to plasterboard, do not use them to hold anything heavy.

Solid walls: Drill a hole for the screw, then plug with a suitable size of fibre or nylon wallplug to give a good grip.
Hollow walls: Screw the brackets into load-bearing struts. Timber uprights (studs) are usually 40 cm–45 cm (16 in–18 in) apart, covered with plasterboard. To find them, either tap along the wall with a hammer or use a bradawl. Various wallplugs and toggles are available for hollow walls. Some expand to grip the inside of the wall when the screw is in place, while others have arms which drop down when the bolt is through.

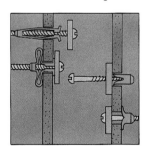

CURING A STICKING DOOR

Several problems may prevent a door from closing properly. They are usually quite simple to deal with.

LOOSE HINGES

● Never move hinges to a different position.
● If the screws won't tighten, use larger ones. Alternatively, wedge the door open at right angles to the frame, remove the screws, fill screw holes with plastic wood and when it has hardened screw them back in firmly.
● If the hinges have become too deeply recessed in the wood, unscrew the deeper side, slip a piece of card behind it and screw back again.

● If the recesses are too shallow, deepen them slightly with a wood chisel.

STIFF HINGES

Metal hinges Apply a drop of oil at the top.
Nylon hinges Slacken or tighten the screws a little.

SWOLLEN WOOD

1 Unscrew the hinges and take the door off.
2 Smooth the wood down at the hinge side and/or the top until the door will fit the frame – allowing for a new coat of paint to be added.
3 Repaint and replace the door on its hinges.
4 **Note:** Wood is less likely to swell if it is thoroughly painted, particularly along the edges and the base.

WARPED FRAME

1 Find out where the door is sticking either by looking for worn paint, or by chalking the edge and seeing where chalk rubs off when door is closed.
2 Sand or plane the warped wood until the door closes well. Repaint.

LAYERS OF PAINT

Paint may build up over the years to make a door stick.
1 Use a paint stripper to remove all old paint.
2 Sandpaper or plane smooth.
3 Prime and repaint.

FLOOR COVERING TOO DEEP

Replace hinges with rising-butt hinges which will lift the door as it opens and closes. (Note: this will only solve the problem if the floor covering is not laid too close to the door.) Rising-butt hinges are in two parts: one fits to the door, the other to the frame.
1 Unscrew the old hinges.
2 Remove the door. Sand (or saw) part of the inner top corner of the door, to accommodate new hinge. (If about to lay new floor covering, place a strip of wood the same thickness as the new flooring against top of door, to mark a sawing line.)
3 Screw the spindle part of the hinge to the frame and the other part to the door.

4 Repaint door where necessary. If it is still tight, plane door at bottom.

Note: Rising-butt hinges need regular lubrication (just a drop of oil at the top).

ROOF CARE

LOFT INSULATION

Loft insulation usually pays for itself within three years. You may be eligible for a grant. Glass fibre and spun mineral wool, from DIY or hardware shops, are easiest. Use rolls of at least 75 mm (3 in) thick. Use loose fill for filling in awkward spaces or unevenly spaced joists. When covering pipes and working in the eaves, lay cardboard or building paper first.

Tools and materials

Insulating material, small saw, scissors, torch or inspection lamp, long extension lead, piece of wood for pressing material into corners.
● If using glass fibre, wear gloves and a mask.

● Take accurate measurements of space between joists, lengths of joists and the number of spaces between.
● Note size of water tank and length and size of pipes.
● Span joists with wide board to act as working platform.
● Unwrap rolls in loft and work gently to prevent loose fibres blowing about.
● Cut material to fit space between joists and press down to fit snugly.
● Check for frayed wiring and don't cover wiring with insulation.
● Lay insulation *over* pipes, not under them.

● Don't insulate the space under the water tank.
● Rinse hands in cold water before washing, to reduce irritation.

SLATES AND TILES

● Check the roof for any broken slates and tiles that need replacing.
● Slates are secured with strips of lead nailed to the roof batten.

● When sliding new slate in place keep it flat against batten, then hook lead over slate end.

● Tiles may be nailed on to roof batten, or may have 'nibs' which fit over battens.
● Check battens before laying new slates or tiles.
● Hinge up overlapping tiles or slates while working and then hinge down again gently over the new one.

FLAT ROOFS

Note: Good-quality materials are essential for flat roofs because of drainage problems. A flat roof may leak because the covering is cracked by heat or movement of timbers.
● Wear soft-soled shoes when working on roof.
● Remove damaged felt and check all boards.

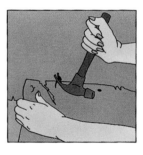

● Sweep roof before and after laying underlay and felt.
● After repair, coat roof with mastic and sprinkle white chippings over to reflect heat.
● Stagger successive layers of felt.

FLASHINGS

These are strips of waterproof material shaped to fit the angle between wall and roof. Zinc is cheap and durable; use it to replace old mortar flashing in the roof/wall angle. Block gutter outlet with old rag before removing mortar flashing, to keep out debris.

GUTTERS AND GULLEYS

SAFETY RULES

- Use a sound ladder, firmly and securely placed.
- Stand ladder on hardboard or chipboard so it won't slip.
- Check ladder extension is firmly fixed.
- Ladder should reach at least 1 m (3.3 ft) above the highest level at which you want to stand.
- Never stand above the third highest rung.
- Don't lean over the side of the ladder as you work.
- Wear soft-soled shoes with good grip.

CLEANING GUTTERS

1 Clear debris (birds' nests, leaves, moss etc) by scraping gutters with a trowel (debris makes good compost).

2 Hose gutter down if necessary.
3 Check all gutters and downpipes are in good structural condition.
4 Mend minor cracks with waterproof tape.

MENDING SAGGING GUTTERS

1 Stretch a length of string along gutter top.
2 Hold spirit level flush with string and check gutter slopes evenly to downpipe.
3 If there's a slight sag, hammer nails into fascia near the outlet, 25 mm (1 in) below the gutter.

4 Drop gutter to new nails.
5 Make pilot holes for screws with a bradawl. Screw gutter into place.
6 Pour water through and check slope of gutter.
7 Fill holes, prime and paint.

SECURING LOOSE DOWNPIPES

1 Lever nails from lowest bracket with claw hammer. Take off downpipe section. Carry on in sections until you reach loose bracket.

2 Make softwood plugs, a little larger and thicker than the holes, and press into holes.

3 Replace downpipe and drive nails through lugs into softwood plugs.
4 If joints between downpipe sections are loose, pack them with proprietary mastic and seal with bitumen paint.

GULLEYS

A gulley is an open rainwater drain in the ground, with a grid. Gulleys should be cleared regularly.
1 Scoop out all the old leaves, silt and mud.
2 Wash out the grid with an old scrubbing or washing-up brush.

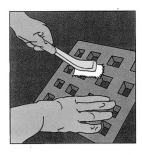

3 Pour a bucket of water down the gulley.

SANDING FLOORBOARDS

Note: it is advisable to wear a dust mask while sanding. Buy a pack of disposable masks from DIY suppliers. If you are sanding an upstairs room, remember the dust will settle on the floor below, so you should remove or cover furniture there too. Be considerate to neighbours – tell them what you are doing and use the sander at a reasonable hour. If you have a leasehold property, check that you are allowed to carry out the work.

Tools and materials
Large floor sander (from hire shops); medium and fine-grade sandpaper (available with sander); handscraper or sanding attachment of electric drill for edges and corners; hammer; gloss or matt seal, varnish or wood stain.

1 **Try to get all furniture** and shelving out of the room – sanding produces a lot of dust, even with a dust bag.

2 **Hammer in nails** well below the surface. Split or damaged boards should be replaced. If there are wide gaps, fill with newspaper and wood filler or papier-mâché, or wood slivers.

3 **Use coarse abrasive paper** in the machine to begin (stiff abrasive paper can be rolled in your hands until it becomes easier to fit into the machine). Before switching on, tilt the sander backwards to lift the drum off the floor. Switch on and lower the machine gently. Keep it moving; keep the cable out of the way by running it over your shoulder. Work slowly and evenly and keep control of the machine – it will try to run away with you.

4 **If floor is badly damaged**, go over it diagonally for the first couple of times and then go in the direction of the boards. DO NOT sand at right-angles to the boards.

5 **Lift drum off the floor** approximately 1 m (3 ft) before you reach the wall, lower it and pull the sander back along the length you have just done. Always lift the drum before turning for the next stretch.

SEALING

1 **Vacuum thoroughly** before beginning to apply your varnish or seal.

2 **Apply the first coat** with a lint-free cloth or sponge or a paint roller, to make sure it sinks into the boards. Subsequent coats can be applied with a brush. Apply two coats in rooms which will have rugs or carpets, and three in hard-worked areas such as the hall or kitchen.

FLOOR MAINTENANCE

MOVING A STAIR CARPET

Stair carpets moved from time to time will wear more evenly. Use one-piece carpet grippers, available in three lengths.

1 Take up the carpet.
2 Nail the carpet grippers into the angle of each step.
3 Starting at the top, move the carpet down about 75 mm (3 in) from its old position and tack it into place on the riser.
4 A fitting tool should be provided to help you press the carpet firmly on to the gripper pins. Pull it taut over the step, down the riser and on to the next gripper pins, until you reach the bottom.
5 Turn in the surplus at the bottom and tack it under.

The carpet can be lifted and laid again whenever necessary. (Move it up or down according to where you have more surplus.)

PATCHING FITTED CARPET OR LINOLEUM

Tools and materials

Small piece of lining paper; latex carpet adhesive – Copydex is good; DIY knife or sharp scissors; spare carpet; hessian.

1 These have to be patched in situ, from the top. Cut out the patch and the damaged piece together (see step 2 of **Patching a Rug**).
2 Cut a piece of paper slightly larger than the patch and push it through the hole to lie flat on the floor or underfelt.
3 Cut a piece of hessian smaller than the paper but slightly larger than the hole and push it through the hole to lie on top of the paper.
4 Paste latex adhesive on the exposed piece of hessian.
5 Put the patch in position and tap round the edges with a hammer to make sure it bonds.

PATCHING VINYL FLOORING

Tools and materials

*Heavy-duty, double-sided adhesive tape (eg Copydex Heavy Duty Double Sided); other items as for **Patching a Rug**.*

1 Lift the vinyl and work from underneath. Brush and vacuum both vinyl and floor well.
2 Cut out the patch and the damaged piece together (see step 2 of **Patching a Rug**).
3 Use tape to fix the underside of the patch and the back of the main piece of vinyl to the floor.

PATCHING A RUG

Tools and materials

Latex carpet adhesive – Copydex is good; DIY knife or sharp scissors; spare carpet; hessian.

1 Use a piece of leftover carpet or take a piece from a hidden area under the bed or another large piece of furniture.
2 Lay the piece on top of the damaged carpet, matching up pattern, pile or grain, and cut through both together with a DIY knife or sharp scissors.
3 Stop any fraying by putting latex adhesive along the edges of hole and patch to halfway up the pile. Leave to dry until semi-transparent.
4 Fit the patch into the hole.
5 Cut a piece of hessian slightly larger than the patch, turn the rug over and stick the hessian over the back with latex adhesive. Tap with a hammer to make sure it sticks.

BINDING MATTING

Sisal, cord and coconut matting will fray at the edges unless they have a satisfactory latex border on both sides of the matting. You can bind any small rug or carpet this way, but ensure it is completely clean, or adhesive won't stick.

Tools and materials

75 mm (3 in) binding tape; a tube of latex carpet adhesive (eg Copydex); DIY knife or sharp scissors.

1 Trim the edges with a DIY knife or sharp scissors.
2 Cut the tape to the required length and squeeze or paint the latex adhesive along half the width of the tape and to the same width along one edge of the matting. When nearly dry, stick the two coated sides together.
3 Turn the matting over and repeat the process with the other half of the tape.
4 Tap along both sides with a hammer to make sure it bonds.

KNOW YOUR OWN FUSE BOX

Electricity comes into the house via a mains cable to the Electricity Board's sealed meter and then to a 'consumer unit' (consisting of your mains switch and fuse box). It is illegal and dangerous to tamper with the sealed meter.

A typical consumer unit contains six fuse carriers: a 30-amp or 45-amp fuse for the cooker, two 30-amp fuses for socket outlet ring circuits, a 15-amp fuse for a hot-water immersion heater and two 5-amp fuses for upstairs and downstairs lighting circuits.

In the ring circuit (ring-main) system, a cable runs from the fuse box around the house, linking sockets and ending back at the fuse box. There may be more than one ring circuit in your house, although each one must have its own 30-amp fuse. Ceiling and fixed wall lights are always on a separate 5-amp circuit.

Some older houses do not have consumer units. Instead they have a separate mains switch for cooker, lighting, water-heating and perhaps a mains switch and multi-way fuse board for power sockets. Remember that, if your wiring is more than 25 years old, it is recommended that you have it checked by a qualified electrical contractor.

FUSES

● If there's a fault, the fuse being the weakest link will 'blow' first, breaking the electrical circuit and minimising the risk of fire.
● Always use fuse wire of the correct amp rating.
● Some fuse boxes have mains circuit-breakers instead of fuses which switch off the supply if there's a fault. Others use cartridge fuses rather than a rewirable fuse carrier.
● Keep torch near fuse box with wire cutters, screwdriver and spare fuse wire: 5-amp for lighting, 30-amp for power circuits and 3- and 13-amp cartridge fuses for plugs.

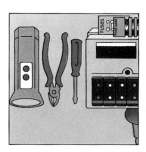

CIRCUIT FAILURE

A failure in several lights or fittings at once means that one of the circuit fuses has blown in the mains fuse box. The cause may be a faulty socket, plug or appliance, an overloading of the circuit, or a fault in the actual wiring of the circuit.

● To rewire a blown fuse: Remove the old wire and any blobs of metal, loop the new wire clockwise round the screw at one end, pass it through the holder and loop it clockwise round the screw at the other end.

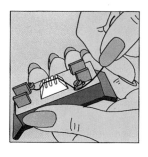

● If a circuit-breaker fuse has 'tripped' (switched off), just switch it on again, once you have sorted out the problem.
● In the case of a cartridge-type mains circuit fuse, simply replace with a new fuse.

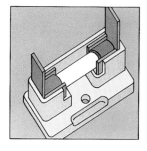

WHAT'S BEHIND YOUR WALLS?

All homes consist of a network of wires, pipes and cables, mostly hidden in the walls or under the floors. If you are pulling down walls, knocking in nails and so on, always check there is no danger of damaging any cables and pipes, to avoid the risk of water/gas leaks and electrocution.

ELECTRICITY

● If you are hammering into walls and you're not sure where the wiring runs, turn the electricity off at the mains.
● Establish where the main fuse box and meter are. Electricity comes into your home to the 'service head' – a sealed unit (which you are not allowed to interfere with) containing the main fuse that protects the whole system. From there single core cables run to your meter. You should be able to tell where the cables run by the positioning of your meter and of the various electrical sockets. This is usually behind the wainscot near the floor and running from socket to socket.

Wiring for lights usually runs behind the ceiling and from there down or along to the light fittings.
● Take extra care if there has been a separate cable put in later – to a cooker for example – especially if it wasn't laid by a professional.

Equally, if you arrive in a new home and find light wires sticking out of the walls, they may still be live so don't start pulling them out or fixing new light fittings until you have turned the power off at the mains.

WATER PIPES

Although actual layout does vary from home to home, most domestic plumbing systems work in the same way and run along similar routes. The plumbing system consists of a network of pipes which carry hot and cold water around your home and also separate pipes for the central heating system.
● Check where the tank is and trace the path of the pipes to the bathroom, toilet, outside tap and so on.
● Check where the boiler is and trace the pipes to and from all the radiators – they usually run under the floorboards.
● In older homes, especially converted ones, there may be mysterious pipes running up through ceilings into flats above. If in doubt, call a plumber to help discover what is connected to what.
● Get to know where the stop cocks and valves are in case of emergencies.

Note: An underground service pipe runs from the water main into each building. Somewhere along this pipe is the water authority's stop cock. All water pipes and stop cocks your side of this are your responsibility. Find out where they are before you move into your home and before you are faced with an emergency. There should be a stop cock near the entry point of the supply to the house, another near the cold water cistern and another near the hot water cylinder. If there aren't, it may be worth installing them.

GAS PIPES

Gas comes into your home through large pipes. From the meter it may be carried to the boiler, fire, cooker and so on, through smaller pipes which probably run under the floorboards.

● If lifting or hammering floorboards, always tackle them with caution. Don't hammer large nails into them without first lifting at least one to find out where the pipes may be running.

QUICK CONVERSION

LENGTHS

- To convert feet to centimetres multiply by 30.48.
- To convert centimetres to feet divide by 30.48.
- To convert yards to metres multiply by 0.9144.
- To convert metres to yards divide by 0.9144.

IMPERIAL	METRIC
$\frac{1}{4}$ in	5 mm
$\frac{1}{2}$ in	1 cm
1 in	2.5 cm
2 in	5 cm
3 in	7 cm
4 in	10 cm
5 in	12 cm
6 in	15 cm
7 in	18 cm
8 in	20 cm
9 in	23 cm
10 in	25 cm
11 in	28 cm
12 in (1 ft)	30 cm
36 in	91 cm
39 in	1 m
10 ft	3.05 m

FABRIC WIDTHS

Fabric widths are sold by the metre in standard widths of:
90 cm (36 in) 140 cm (55 in)
115 cm (45 in) 150 cm (60 in)

TEMPERATURES

- To convert Fahrenheit to centigrade (celsius), subtract 32 and multiply by 0.5555.
- To convert centigrade (celsius) to Fahrenheit, multiply by 1.8 and add 32.

WEIGHTS

- To convert pounds to kilograms multiply by 0.4536.
- To convert kilograms to pounds divide by 0.4536.
- To convert ounces to grams multiply by 28.3495.
- To convert grams to ounces divide by 28.3495.

METRIC	IMPERIAL
5 g	$\frac{1}{4}$ oz
15 g	$\frac{1}{2}$ oz
25 g	1 oz
50 g	2 oz
85 g	3 oz
110 g	4 oz
140 g	5 oz
180 g	6 oz
200 g	7 oz
225 g	8 oz
250 g	9 oz
280 g	10 oz
300 g	11 oz
340 g	12 oz
375 g	13 oz
400 g	14 oz
425 g	15 oz
450 g	16 oz (1 lb)
1 kilogram	2.2 lb

OVEN TEMPERATURES

ELECTRIC		GAS	SOLID FUEL
°C	°F		
70	150		
80	175		
100	200	Low	
110	225	$\frac{1}{4}$	
120	250	$\frac{1}{2}$	Very cool
140	275	1	Cool
150	300	2	
160	325	3	Slow
180	350	4	Moderate
190	375	5	
200	400	6	Moderately hot
220	425	7	Hot
230	450	8	Very hot
240	475	9	Very hot

Figures on tables have been rounded up slightly to make them easier to compare.

LIQUIDS

- To convert UK pints to litres multiply by 0.568.
- To convert USA pints to litres multiply by 0.473.
- To convert litres to UK pints divide by 0.568.
- To convert litres to USA pints divide by 0.473.

METRIC	IMPERIAL	USA
5 ml	$\frac{1}{8}$ fl oz	1 tsp
15 ml	$\frac{1}{2}$ fl oz	1 tbsp
25 ml	1 fl oz	$\frac{1}{8}$ cup
50 ml	2 fl oz	$\frac{1}{4}$ cup
65 ml	$2\frac{1}{2}$ fl oz	$\frac{1}{3}$ cup
100 ml	4 fl oz	$\frac{1}{2}$ cup
150 ml	5 fl oz	$\frac{5}{8}$ cup
175 ml	6 fl oz	$\frac{3}{4}$ cup
225 ml	8 fl oz	1 cup ($\frac{1}{2}$ USA pint)
300 ml	10 fl oz ($\frac{1}{2}$ UK pt)	$1\frac{1}{4}$ cups
350 ml	12 fl oz	$1\frac{1}{2}$ cups
400 ml	14 fl oz	$1\frac{3}{4}$ cups
475 ml	16 fl oz	2 cups (1 USA pt)
600 ml	20 fl oz (1 UK pt)	$2\frac{1}{2}$ cups
750 ml	24 fl oz	3 cups
900 ml	32 fl oz	4 cups (2 USA pt)
1 litre	35 fl oz	$4\frac{1}{4}$ cups
1.14 litres	40 fl oz (2 UK pt)	5 cups

DRILLING GUIDE

● When fixing objects to walls, you need to make a hole in the wall, fill it with plugging compound or a wallplug and then screw into this. The wallplug expands as the screw goes in.

● Accurate drilling is essential for all fixings – inaccuracies will result in loose fixings and non-level surfaces.

Beginners are often advised to use a hand drill, but in fact it can often be easier to start with an electric drill as both hands can guide the drill.

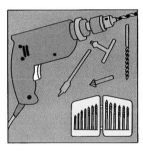

There are three ways of drilling into walls:

1 A masonry drill bit in a brace, breast drill or small hand drill.

2 A masonry drill bit in an electric drill set at either low or high speed.

3 An electric hammer drill fitted with a special type of masonry drill – the hammer drill vibrates the masonry drill in and out.

Masonry drills

There are two types of drill:

1 Those meant for rotary drilling with hand drills and ordinary electric drills. These can be resharpened with a special grinding wheel.

2 Drills for use with 'impact' drilling in hammer drills. These should be resharpened professionally.

WHICH DRILL?

Plaster, plasterboard and hollow walls: any type of drill, including a small hand drill, can be used.

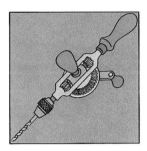

Clinker blocks: have largely replaced breeze blocks for internal walls and are comparatively soft. Use an electric high-speed drill or a hammer drill.

Brick: use an electric high-speed drill (hard work) or a hammer drill.

Concrete: use a hammer drill.

DRILL SIZES

Masonry drills come in numbered sizes linked to the size of screws and traditional fibre wallplugs.

The accompanying table lists the masonry drill sizes in general use with their imperial and metric conversions.

Number	mm	in
6	4	$\frac{5}{32}$
8	4.8	$\frac{3}{16}$
10	5.6	$\frac{7}{32}$
12	6.4	$\frac{1}{4}$
14	7.1	$\frac{9}{32}$
16	7.9	$\frac{5}{16}$
18	8.7	$\frac{11}{32}$
20	9.5	$\frac{3}{8}$

Notes

● Before you start, make a small dent with a bradawl so that you can locate the drill tip.

● If the surface is slippery, put some sticky tape over it.

● To drill a wide hole, it may be easier to drill a narrow one first and then expand it.

● Use a piece of sticky tape on the drill to mark the depth you want to go to.

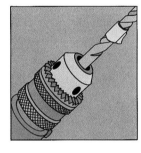

● Keep a steady pressure.

● Hold the drill accurately in line with the direction of the hole (you can buy a tiny spirit level which tells you if you're drilling straight).

● Use white spirit, not oil, to lubricate the drill tip.

● Withdraw the drill frequently to release the brick dust.

● You can drill into the joins between tiles, but not into the joins between bricks.

FOUR

FINISHING TOUCHES

Details make all the difference when it comes to creating a home with a truly individual and special feel. How you display your favourite possessions, the way plants or pictures are grouped together, a collection of objects linked by a common shape or colour – small embellishments like these lift a room out of the ordinary, and turn a house into a much-loved home.

Collections
Paintings and prints
Soft furnishings
Fresh and dried flowers
Pot plants
Table settings

It's the little touches of ingenuity and inspiration that give a home its character. Cleverly chosen pictures, an imaginatively displayed collection, a pile of colour-matched cushions, a mass of glorious green pot plants or a basketful of subtle dried flowers – items like these needn't cost a fortune, but can fill a simple room with fascinating clues about its owner's personality.

Treasures on display

You might be a born magpie, with all sorts of beautiful bits and pieces to put on show. Or perhaps you just have one or two eye-catching items that you want to display to maximum effect. Either way, you'll get the most impact by grouping your collection all together, rather than spreading it round the house.

Small items, such as thimbles or teaspoons, need a dark background to show them off. A polished wooden tray would do the job, and could be moved every now and then to a different spot in the room. Re-arrange your collections from time to time to give them fresh emphasis.

Matching rows of mugs and cups hang or stand in orderly fashion, while a miscellaneous collection of over-sized cups and saucers marches around the room at ceiling height.

Larger pieces of china, glassware or pottery might merit their own set of display shelves. These could be purpose-built, in sections sized to fit each individual piece, although if your collection is still growing, ordinary open shelves could give more flexibility. Good lighting is vital, especially for glass.

Put your collection where it can be easily admired and, if the items are not too fragile, encourage people to handle them. You could keep a little 'log-book', listing details of how each piece was acquired, for interested visitors to browse through.

Wherever you decide to display a collection, give some thought to how it is arranged, and experiment with different effects. Some pieces look good lined in order of height, or fanning out from a central, striking object. Or you could link adjacent pieces, grouping them according to colour, shape or pattern.

Of course there's no need for a collection to stick to one type of object. You could collect around a colour scheme: blue-and-white china is one of the most traditional and attractive ideas. Or pick a theme – flowers, ducks, ships – and gather together appropriate ornaments, pictures, pieces of fabric. The only limit to the possibilities is your imagination.

Far left: Vivid colours and strong shapes are the hallmarks of a collection of period china. Simple shelves and a plain cream background allow the pieces to speak for themselves.

A mass of blue and white china crowds the dresser, while an attractive assortment of baskets in all shapes and sizes is huddled high on a beam.

check point

Paintings

The most common types are: Oil, Watercolour, Gouache, Tempera, Acrylic. The name refers to the type of paint used.

Prints

An original print will always be described by the printing method used to produce it.

Woodcut, Wood engraving, Linocut All types of 'Relief Printing'. The artist gouges away areas of a wood or lino block and the remaining raised areas are coated with ink. The block is pressed on to paper to form the image.

Etching, Engraving Both types of 'Intaglio Printing'. The image is cut into a metal plate which is coated with ink. A press forces ink from the crevices on the plate to print an image on paper.

Drypoint, Mezzotint, Aquatint Variations on the Intaglio process.

Lithograph The printing image is drawn on a flat surface and made ink-receptive, while the non-printing areas are made ink-repellent. The inked image is pressed on to paper.

Screenprint Ink is forced through a stencil which is fixed to a mesh screen tightly stretched over a frame.

Picture sense

Almost any home you enter will have pictures on the walls – whether they are family photographs, unframed posters, or priceless oils.

By all means buy pictures which tone with the colour scheme in the room where you plan to hang them. But don't stick too slavishly to your chosen colour palette, otherwise you risk the picture 'disappearing' into its surroundings. A striking contrast will ensure that the picture is noticed, and that it will continue to make an impact even when you have owned it for some time.

Most people buy pictures on impulse. That's fine for inexpensive posters or reproductions, but a slightly different matter for original paintings or prints, when one glance at the price tag might make you beat a hasty retreat from the shop. If the picture represents a sizeable investment, ask yourself 'Is it worth it?'. The answer is probably yes, if you really like the picture, for a combination of reasons.

● A picture can add life and colour to an otherwise blank wall, and a pleasing image makes up for a lack of views from windows.
● A print or painting will give you pleasure for many years and may well appreciate in value.
● Many galleries will let you pay by instalments, so you can spread the cost over three or six months.

Buying from galleries For originals, rather than reproduction prints, you will usually need to visit a gallery. Many people feel intimidated by the thought of walking into a gallery, worrying that everything will be too expensive and that they will be pressured into buying. By and large these fears are ill-founded. Most galleries are very approachable nowadays, and welcome browsers. They will offer advice if you ask for it, but will otherwise leave you free to look around. Many galleries stock smaller, less expensive items such as pottery and glassware. You don't have to spend too much, nor do you need to feel guilty about leaving empty-handed.

Local galleries will usually hold special exhibitions with a particular theme or to promote the work of one artist. These are worth looking out for if you are keen on, say, river scenes or animal paintings, or have a favourite artist whose work you would like to collect.

Emphatic geometrical lines in the picture are thoroughly in keeping with the architecture of this room.

Six pictures are hung very close together to form a solid block of design just the right size for the wall it occupies.

Distinctive soft furnishings

Cushions are one of the easiest and cheapest ways to brighten up faded furniture and add fresh colour to a room which you cannot afford to redecorate. But select them carefully, with an eye to the overall effect. Choose a mixture of different shapes and sizes, but use a theme to bring the look together – bold floral prints; designs featuring animals; muted tartans or checks; traditional needle-point patterns.

Frills and flowers are the theme for this comfortable window seat. One or two plain cushions pick up the main colours from the scheme.

Lively animals bound
across the patterned
cushions, while larger
pillows in autumnal gold
echo the rich colours of
the sofa.

Bedding in a vibrant jungle print is a perfect foil for the plain leaf green walls. Black headboard and furniture make the colours glow even more brightly.

Add instant interest to a plain sofa with a brightly patterned fabric 'throw' slung over the back. Or introduce a round table draped with a patterned fabric which co-ordinates with your other furnishings, or covered with a plain colour and topped off prettily with a smaller piece of lace. You can also use lace mats and runners to soften dark wood sideboards and dressing tables in period-style rooms. And a striking patchwork quilt lends warmth and rustic charm to any scheme, and looks just as effective hung on the wall as covering the bed.

Right: Ribbons and bows give way to lilac-coloured blossoms on a two-tiered cloth. Don't skimp on fabric, otherwise the drape loses its generous full effect.

Far right: Cheerful red and white, used in a selection of small flower prints for a handsome, colonial-style patchwork quilt. The rest of the decor is deliberately kept plain.

Angular lilies, although beautiful, can look stark. Here, they are offset with an arrangement of softer blooms, made especially light and airy with a few sprigs of delicate gypsophila.

Far right: Glass vases in glowing jewel colours deserve the most lavish and showy flowers. Even the stems become part of the arrangement in a translucent container, which needs to stand in a light position to be seen at its best.

Flower arrangements

Fresh flowers You can change fresh flower arrangements every week to follow the seasons or your mood. Use your imagination when it comes to choosing a container. Equip yourself with a collection of vases in glass and pottery, choosing simple designs and colours which won't overpower the flowers, and wide necks for easier arranging. But consider also using jugs and jars, dishes, carafes, bottles and glasses that you already have in the kitchen. Any of these could make a sympathetic container.

Use flowers as lavishly as you can afford, and choose a container which makes the most of the blooms you have. Meagre bunches can look 'lost' if arranged loosely in a large vase, and will have far more impact packed in closely. Cut the stems down to achieve this if necessary, and add foliage to fill in the gaps.

Choose colours sensitively. Flowers which echo the colours of the room will always work well, or you can be more adventurous and go for a striking contrast. Different types of flower linked by colour – all white, or all pink, say – will look effective together.

Delightfully dusky shades of old gold and moss green which feature in the flower arrangement are subtly reiterated in its wicker container.

Another way to guarantee success is to make an arrangement using the same flower in different shades of one colour, such as roses in yellow, cream and white.

The size and type of arrangement depends on where the flowers are to be placed. Choose low arrangements for dinner tables, where it's important not to obstruct the diners' view; or for low shelves or tables, where they will be seen from above. Put tall, wide arrangements where they will be viewed from a distance: on a table at the end of a hall, for instance.

Dried flowers These can form a more permanent part of your decor, although it's a good idea to 'refresh' arrangements periodically by removing any blooms which are looking dusty or dishevelled, and replacing them with new flowers.

Go for containers in warm-looking natural materials – wicker baskets, copperware or terracotta pots are ideal. Anchor your arrangements in special foam or wire and mass the flowers together thickly to make the most of their delightful colours and textures and to hide the twiggy-looking dried stems.

Use dried flowers wherever you want to give a touch of soft colour to a room. A big basket of flowers and leaves fills a blank fireplace in summer; a tiny arrangement of rosebuds adds a nostalgic note to a romantic bedroom; a wicker punnet of brilliant marigolds livens up a dark bathroom where real flowers would not flourish.

Far right: Filling a corner with everlasting flowers, this bulbous terracotta pot holds a huge cloud of fragile dried blooms.

check point

Plants for cool, dark rooms

Fatshedera (Ivy tree) Easy to grow. Water well in summer. Pinch out tops to keep bushy shape.

Philodendron Scandens (Sweetheart vine) Rampant climber with attractive, heart-shaped leaves. Keep out of draughts.

Plants for sunny windowsills

Beloperone Guttata (Shrimp plant) Needs sunlight to produce salmon-pink flower heads. Prune in spring.

Pelargonium (Geranium) Flowers abundantly from late spring well into autumn. Remove dead flowers regularly.

Plants which can tolerate central heating

Chlorophytum (Spider plant) Grass-like leaves which fall gracefully. Puts out tiny plantlets on long, arching stems. Keep well watered in summer.

Clivia (Kaffir lily) Upright plant with large, orange or red funnel-shaped flowers appearing in late spring. Keep out of direct sunlight.

Plants which are easy to grow

Hedera (Ivy) Can be used as a climber or trailer. Many different varieties, some with variegated leaves.

Monstera Deliciosa (Swiss Cheese plant) Tree-like plant with deeply cut and perforated leaves. Can grow to a very large size.

Pot plant magic

Thriving greenery in pots lasts far longer than fresh flowers and will change gradually as it grows. Plants are usually happier, and look better, grouped together, their pots disguised with planters or jardinieres. Several large plants can stand together on the floor, with smaller plants added on a shelf or table behind.

Mix the types of plants, placing upright varieties next to lush, bushy types; and letting a climber creep up the wall behind, or a

All plants appreciate light, so shelves straddling a window with an uninspiring view make the perfect home for a few favourite specimens.

One huge plant is worth half-a-dozen smaller ones when it comes to sheer impact. Make sure a bathroom has a suitable source of natural light before filling it with greenery.

trailer hang down from above to produce an attractive mass of different leaves. But do remember that your plants will need a certain amount of tender loving care in order to survive, and arrange for them to be looked after if you are going away for more than a few days.

Keep plants looking their best by removing dead leaves regularly. Spruce up dusty foliage by wiping gently with a damp cloth and treating with spray-on 'shine'.

A crisp white cloth topping one in rich maroon makes the final effect less formal. As an alternative, a cream lace cloth over the darker fabric would lighten the mood and give a pretty finishing touch.

Stylish table settings

Entertaining, even if it's just a simple meal for a few friends, gives you a chance to spread the table with style. A tablecloth is almost always essential to protect – or disguise – the surface beneath. White linen or heavy cotton damask are traditional and the perfect foil for patterned or plain china. Bear in mind, however, that every stain will show, and these cloths need careful washing and starching to keep them in top condition.

The way you set the table can have a surprisingly strong effect on the mood of the gathering. For example, to create an intimate feel for a winter dinner party, use a tablecloth in a dark colour like

maroon or forest green, offset with glowing, polished cutlery and the warm shades of natural earthenware plates. In summer, alter the scene dramatically using a pastel pink or flower-embroidered cloth, and delicate china in ivory or pure white.

You may like to collect more than one set of china: a robust design for everyday use and a finer, more elegant service for entertaining (see Choosing china and glass, page 29, for guidance). For a more informal look, you could put together a miscellany of plates and bowls from different sources, matching them in size and theme: floral designs, willow pattern, or country scenes would all be fairly easy to find.

The finishing touch for your table should be an eye-catching centrepiece: a patterned bowl piled with polished red apples; a silvery tray edged with greenery and filled with tangerines and nuts; half-a-dozen candles at different heights, in colours to match the setting.

All important details

The accessories in your home, although tiny in themselves, add up to a powerful image. Every element, from lightshades to door-knobs, towel rails to shelf brackets, has something to contribute.

But don't worry if you're faced with the prospect of gradually creating the home you *really* want, over a period of years. You can easily produce attractive and original effects by thoughtful juxtaposition of items that you probably already own.

For instance, a carefully placed mirror immediately doubles the impact of anything in front or opposite: hang one on the wall facing a window for extra light, or put one above a shelf or mantelpiece and front it with flowers or a row of distinctively shaped ornaments. A ticking clock is a soothing addition to a room where you want to feel calmed. Hang photo portraits of close relatives in ascending order of age up the wall alongside the stairs, to make a fascinating family gallery. Don't hide away any acquisitions which please your eye, even if they were not originally intended to be decorative, but use them to exhibit your own individual tastes and preferences. The permutations are limitless and the final product – a welcoming home, with a really personal feel – endlessly satisfying.

Jolly vases in brilliant colours picked straight from a child's paint box call for flowers chosen purely for fun.

Position flowers intended to reflect into the room so that both sides of the vase have equal weight of blooms. This ensures that the arrangement looks good from all angles.

FIVE

HOME WISE

Safety at home is of prime importance. Children's rooms call for special care in planning, while other areas of the house are covered in a useful safety checklist. There's advice on security too, from locks and bolts to burglar alarms. Also in this chapter you'll find advice on another area of concern to homeowners: how to capitalise on a property's potential value by making wise improvements. And finally, there are helpful guidelines on hiring help without giving yourself a headache.

Safety is a vital factor in planning a child's room that will graduate comfortably from imaginative nursery to teenage den. And, of course, it's also important to make the rest of the house into a hazard-free environment for children and adults alike. A thorough check of security precautions to protect your home against intruders is also advisable.

Remember that children develop rapidly, and a feature that is safe one day may become a hazard the next.

KEEP SAFE

Nurseries
Children's rooms
Safety check list
Crime prevention
Locks and bolts • Burglar alarms

Casualty departments throughout the country deal with thousands of small victims of home accidents each year, and at least 160 annually die from their injuries. A child's strength and daring often comes as a surprise to parents. Once a child is mobile, he or she is capable of clambering out on to a window ledge, pulling over a hefty bookcase, or 'escaping' from the house and into possible danger outside, the minute your back is turned.

It *is* possible to provide a safe environment for children to sleep and play in, but you will need to adapt your ideas and furnishing techniques right from the start.

Nursery planning

Buy a washable paint intended for a nursery, which means that it will be lead free. Position eye-catching wallpaper friezes safely out of reach, where they can't be picked away from the wall. If you have any second-hand item you are thinking about putting in a child's bedroom, it may have lead paint on it, especially if it is quite old. Very young children often chew on furniture. For safety's sake strip it completely and repaint it.

Make sure that any second-hand furniture you buy conforms to current safety standards. The standards for babies' cots, for instance, are constantly being revised, so it's generally best to buy new if you can, checking that the item you have chosen complies to British Standards.

Once your baby moves into a bed, fit a secure safety rail on to the side. Such a rail is just as important for older children too, especially if you have bunk beds. The top bunk shouldn't be used for children under the age of six, and even then you need to ensure that the ladder is secure.

Light and sound

Most bedrooms have only one or two electric sockets – not nearly enough to cope with today's electronically minded child. Music centres, computers, TVs and desk lights all need a socket of their own. Never take the risk of overloading sockets. Make a point of putting in a few extra when your child's room is redecorated. Until your child is old enough to understand the dangers, make sure all socket outlets have safety covers.

It's a good idea to choose wall lights rather than bedside lamps, as trailing flexes are always a danger. A dimmer switch for the main light is useful, especially for tiny children afraid of the dark, or for new parents still coping with night feeds, when a bright light is unnecessary.

Many parents don't appreciate that a radiator can become hot enough to hurt a child's delicate skin. Fit guards that totally enclose the radiators in a child's room and, of course, always use a fireguard on open fires anywhere in the house.

Stepping out of the nursery

Once a child can toddle, you'll need to fit a safety gate at the top of the stairs. Keep it closed all the time, even at night. Children often wake earlier than the rest of the family, and might go exploring. You could also fit a gate at the bottom of the stairs, to prevent a child from risking a fall by climbing upstairs. When the child is older, you could consider fitting a handrail at 'child-level', especially if your stairs are steep.

Windows are all too tempting to children with an adventurous streak, even those who ought to be old enough to know better. Don't put any item of furniture under the window where it could be climbed on to make a handy 'step' on to the sill. Fit locking window catches and put safety film or vertical bars over the glass. Do make sure though, that any of these devices are simply and quickly removable in an emergency, such as a fire.

Store toys in a basket or choose a box with slam-proof hinges. A simple safety test is to drop the lid shut on a pencil and see how much damage it does. Fit slam-proof hinges on all heavy doors in the house, as well.

Screw free-standing furniture into the wall. Shelves provided for displaying a child's treasures should always be within easy reach, so there's no temptation to start climbing. Children are naturally curious, and will always be tempted to investigate an

Far right: A simple barricade keeps toddlers out of the kitchen, but still in sight of adults.

intriguing object that's just out of reach. Beware of putting heavy objects where they might topple down on to a child, and make sure too that items like televisions are well secured.

Try to avoid furniture with sharp edges and corners. Otherwise, fit the corners with special pads to soften them. You'll probably want to use a material that's easy to clean on the floor of a child's room, such as cushioned vinyl or cork. If you add a washable rug for warmth, make sure you fit the edges with non-slip adhesive strips.

Play safe

Many accidents, particularly to older children, are a result of play sessions getting out of hand. Make sure that children understand the dangers of throwing bats or sticks. Even an empty swing seat can become a dangerous missile. Broken toys should be removed and disposed of safely.

From birth to 1

● Never leave a baby lying on a chair or sofa.
● Keep hot drinks out of reach. Be careful if the baby is on your lap while you drink a cup of tea or coffee.
● Fires must be well-guarded.

From 1 to 2

● Fit a secure gate on the stairs and slam-proof hinges to the doors.
● Toxic substances like medicines, cleaning products, pesticides etc must be kept locked up.
● Fit a pan guard to the cooker and keep toddlers out of the way when cooking.

From 2 to 3

● Keep matches, scissors and sewing equipment hidden.
● Make sure that items you want to keep out of a child's reach are still inaccessible.
● Don't leave power tools where a child could play with them.

From 3 to 5

● Insist that boisterous games take place away from windows and glass doors.
● Even heavy items, like lawnmowers, could be dangerous to a curious child. Keep them locked away and warn your child not to copy you when you use them.
● Tell your child where he or she may and may not go without you. Give frequent reminders.

SAFETY CHECK

How safe is your home? Check through this list of common safety pitfalls and find out what precautions you can take to make your home a safer place to live in – for everyone.

The kitchen

● Keep knives and sharp utensils in drawers or cabinets, not on work surfaces.

● Always slice vegetables downwards on a flat surface, keeping hands behind the cutting edge of the knife.

● Watch for over-heating when deep-frying. The pan should be no more than one-third full of fat, after the food has been added.

● Make sure there are plenty of electric power points for appliances, and never overload them. The total load on any single socket should not exceed 13 amps.

● Avoid trailing flexes to irons, food processors etc.

● Put empty cans safely into a closed rubbish bin.

● Plan your kitchen so that you have plenty of workspace near cooker and sink.

● Use non-slip floorings and clean up spills immediately.

● Have microwaves serviced regularly.

● Keep children away from the cooking area and take extra care when preparing hot drinks or soup – they could easily get scalded.

● Keep items in daily use within easy reach, not on high shelves.

The bathroom

● Non-slip bath and floor mats are a simple but effective way to prevent falls.

● A hand-rail by the bath is advisable, especially for older people.

● Three-pin sockets and flick light switches *inside* the bathroom are extremely dangerous. Pull cords are by far the best sort of light switch to use, as they are safe to handle with wet hands.

● Keep medicines clearly labelled in a lockable cabinet.

● Stay with children at all times when they are in the bath. A child can drown in a few inches of water.

● Showers should be fitted with an anti-scald device, and an isolation switch if electric.

● All hot pipework should be concealed or out of reach.

● Wall-mounted electric heaters should be sited at least 2 m (6 ft) above the floor.

Floorings

● Use non-slip backing with loose carpets and rugs, especially on polished floorings or parquet.

● Do not lay rugs near glass doors or windows, where tripping could have serious consequences.

● Make sure that fitted stair carpet is well-secured and kept in good repair.

DIY

● Keep children out of the way when tackling DIY jobs, and put all tools away, out of reach afterwards.

● Stand ladders on firm, level ground, and ask someone to keep the ladder steady at the bottom.

● Don't be tempted to stretch too far when working on a ladder. Move it as often as you need to.

● Keep all chemicals, paints, cleaners, glues etc locked away from children. Label them clearly and keep firmly closed.

● Check that power tools are un-damaged and properly wired *before* you use them.

All round the house

● Fit safety glass, which breaks safely, to patio doors and low level windows.

● Good lighting is essential on stairs, or anywhere in the house where there are steps.

● Windows that a child could reach should be fitted with child-resistant window stays.

● All stairways should have a sturdy handrail.

● Bannisters should be close enough together so that children cannot squeeze through.

Handrails fitted on either side of the bath make getting in and out both safe and easy.

Sharp blades are well-shielded in a knife block which can stand on the worktop or be wall-mounted to keep it out of reach of children.

SAFE AS HOUSES

These days there's a good chance that the average burglar won't wait until dark to come out. He – or, just as likely, she – could well still be at school and will probably be smartly dressed. The one thing we can all be sure about is that most burglars are opportunists. Police figures show that one-third of all household burglaries occur when thieves simply let themselves in through unlocked doors or open windows. What's more, the property owners could be elsewhere in the house when the burglary takes place: watching television in another room, for instance, while the back door is left unlocked.

So, it pays to be meticulous about keeping doors and windows secure at all times. The harder you make it for burglars to get in, the more chance there is of them being disturbed. Each lock or defensive device shortens the odds of them getting caught. But even before you start bolting up your home, there are plenty of other ways you can protect yourself.

Giveaway signs

Take a tip from the old wartime saying about careless talk. Cancelling the papers before you go away is a good idea – but not while the shop is crowded. Gossiping in the pub about an eagerly awaited break could attract the wrong sort of attention.

It also pays to make it look as if someone is at home while you're out or away. Ask a reliable neighbour to clear post and circulars off the doorstep. It helps if they can make the place look occupied by drawing the curtains at night or cutting the grass.

Lighting up time

Leaving lights on and a radio playing can help make the house appear occupied, and there are plenty of easy-to-use time switches which will turn lights and appliances on or off while you're away. You can also buy a device which will switch a light on and off randomly during the night, or switch it on every evening in response to growing darkness.

Outdoor security lighting can either be attached to an outside wall or installed in the garden. Wall lights such as porch lights, bulkheads or illuminated signs are easier to instal, as you can control them from indoors.

Locks and bolts

Consider putting bars at the shed windows if tools and ladders are stored inside, and use a suitable padlock on the door if the wood is too thin for a mortice. The same rules apply to the garage.

Invest in window locks for all windows that are accessible, not just from the ground or roof, but from drainpipes, walls or temporary scaffolding. Fit locks to accessible skylight windows too. You can fix the glass strips of vulnerable louvre windows into their holders with epoxy adhesive, or fit bars over the inside.

Doors need a particularly good lock, especially the 'final' exit door, since you can't bolt this one behind you as you go out. Choose a deadlocking mortice level lock, with five or more levers. Cover the letterbox with a draught excluder or wire letter basket. Have a chain fitted and, if the door is solid, a spy hole. Wood framed French windows offer little resistance unless grilled or barred. Back doors should also be fitted with a good lock.

Alarm advice

Should you have an alarm or not? There are several good reasons for not having one, not least the fact that it makes burglars think you have something worth stealing. In addition, an alarm can be costly to fit, and if you live miles from anywhere no one will hear it. But the mere sight of an alarm can also deter some burglars, which is why some people use dummy boxes. If you decide to invest, make sure you get expert advice.

It pays not to keep anything valuable in the house in the first place. Protect items of great value in a small safe, or take them to the bank. Remember, burglars know all the hiding places, so don't risk keeping any irreplaceable items in the house.

check point

- Most burglaries take place during daylight, in the afternoon.
- Lock away ladders and any tools a burglar might find useful.
- The average burglary takes less than three minutes.
- Large shrubs and fences around the house provide cover for thieves. Fit exterior lighting linked to a time switch or heat-sensitive device triggered by anyone approaching.
- Your local crime prevention officer will give you free advice about home security and can tell you how to mark valuables to make them easier to identify if stolen.
- Never leave keys in the lock or under a mat. A burglar could break a window to reach them, or put a hand through the letterbox or even the cat flap.
- Coat drainpipes with non-drying anti-burglar paint.
- Most homes have about a one-in-25 chance of being burgled in any one year.
- Protect your windows and glass doors with bars and window locks.
- There's less than a one-in-three chance of a burglar being caught, and even less chance of any stolen property being recovered.

Are you wondering whether to convert an attic into a bedroom, add a conservatory or build a garage? It makes financial sense to think carefully before embarking on any major home alterations. Choose your improvements with an eye to the future: some add precious pounds to the value of your property, but others will give a poor return on your investment.

MONEY
matters

Your property's potential

Making market comparisons

Increasing the value

Sound investments

Problem areas

Dos and don'ts

M any of us dream of making major improvements to our homes: a loft conversion to provide an extra bedroom or bathroom; adding on a garage or conservatory; installing double glazing right through the house. But before you embark on any costly work, make sure you will get your money back when you want to sell the property. You might be planning to stay in your home for many years, but the unexpected can always happen: a job offer entailing a move, for instance, or an ailing relative who needs you close at hand.

So, ask yourself one vital question *before* you start building. Would the cost of the work be recovered if the house was sold? Even a modest expenditure should be recoverable in a reasonable period of time. Your first step should be to get a valuation by an established local estate agent, so that you can assess the potential of your scheme.

What are the price raisers?

If you live in a street where some houses have already had lofts converted, for instance, compare a recent sale price of one of these with your own valuation. If the difference is at least the equivalent of the building cost of converting your loft, you could be on to a winner. If you want to convert an adjacent garage into an additional room, find out what effect this would have on your valuation. In areas where off-street parking is at a premium, a garage may be worth more than another room.

Conservatories are often seen as price raisers. But the range of products – and costs – is enormous. What you can afford and

An attic conversion not only makes a useful extra room but, if well done, adds value to your home.

Think carefully about the size and style of a conservatory. The wrong choice could prove expensive when you come to move.

Money spent on the kitchen of your dreams may give you pleasure as long as you live in the house – but could prove a poor investment if you plan to move on.

what the property value can stand may not be the same. It would be easy to over-develop, adding an expensive structure to a relatively ordinary house. And you could just as swiftly spoil a house of distinctive character by putting up something rather too utilitarian in style.

Most estate agents will confirm that a second bathroom or a cloakroom always add value to a house, but expensively re-furbishing an existing one may do nothing at all. Gold-plated taps in a fancy whirlpool bath could be your idea of heaven, but they may not add a jot of value to your home.

Double glazing makes a house more saleable than an identical one without it, but the overall cost of installation may take time and inflation to be absorbed into the value, although the savings on fuel bills will certainly mitigate against the cost.

Do check whether your proposed improvements need planning permission.
Do look at your property objectively. You may not have a car, but garages are good selling points.
Do make sure all improvements blend in with the architecture.
Don't substantially alter the character of a distinctive house.
Don't make improvements beyond the scope of your potential buyers.
Don't make the sort of 'improvement' which can easily knock money *off* the value of your house: stone cladding for example, or replacing original sash windows with tilting plastic ones.
Don't expect to recoup the cost of items which appeal to your particular taste.
Don't over-improve. A terraced house is still a terraced house, whatever you do to it.

Remember what potential buyers are looking for:

● good location – can be more important than the property itself.
● assurance that new roads or estates aren't going to be built nearby.
● reasonable condition – but many buyers are happy to buy a property in need of some renovation.
● manageable size: 3–4 bedrooms is the average preferred size.

Low-return investments

A cupboard installed under the stairs, shelves in the sitting room, expensive wallpaper in the bedroom will all prove to be disappointing investments offering little, if any, return if your prospective buyer doesn't want them.

A well-appointed kitchen helps enormously when it comes to selling a house, but there is a great deal of difference between reaping the benefits of £5000 and trying to recoup £10,000 or even £15,000. Many buyers won't be able to differentiate between one make or another and, even if they could, would not be prepared to reflect your investment in the price they offer.

Expediency plays a part in many improvements. Building a 'granny flat' may be paid for by granny herself. But beware: a high-quality specification may not add the equivalent value to your house. It might be better to invest the same money in trading up to a larger property altogether.

Putting an attic into commission with a retractable ladder may cost quite a bit to do but add little to the market value of the house. Spending a lot more to convert the attic into a whole new storey, approached by a well-designed staircase, could put your house into a different bracket and be worth every penny.

A swimming pool installed in the grounds of a large mansion may cost no more to build than a similar one in the back of a small suburban semi. The former, however, will probably add substantially to the value of the house a few years later, whereas the cost of the latter may never be recovered.

Market value

The golden rule is that for an improvement to be a price raiser, the work you are carrying out must push up the overall market value of the house. This is particularly important to bear in mind if you need to borrow money for the project, but even a simple scheme, financed out of savings, should be realisable as an investment rather than an expenditure.

HIRED HANDS

Who to employ

Making payment

If things go wrong

Advertisements explained

Plumbers • Electricians

Safety pointers

From time to time, most of us decide it's worthwhile paying someone else to do a job in the house for us. The trouble is, we all know someone who has had a bad experience with hired help. Unfortunately, there is nothing to stop people with no training or experience setting up in business as builders, plumbers or electricians.

Protecting yourself

How can you make sure you don't get caught out by unscrupulous cowboys? It's not too difficult to avoid obvious con men. The kind of people who knock at your door and offer to tarmac your drive should be treated with the utmost suspicion, especially if they want paying in advance for 'materials'. Otherwise, it's a question of doing a bit of research before you employ anyone, and making sure you get everything in writing.

Ask around among friends and neighbours for reliable local firms whose work they know and who have a local reputation to protect. Once you have a couple of names, ask the firms to send someone to look at your job. Except for the most trivial tasks, get as much as possible in writing.

The best safeguard is always to get an estimate. Ask for a written, itemised estimate, and add a clause to the effect that you will be consulted if the price has to rise for any reason. Insist, and get written agreement, that any faults that emerge once the work is finished will be fixed within a certain amount of time.

On a large job you may be asked to pay in instalments. Don't part with any money before work is started. If you are really convinced that an advance payment must be made for materials, it

● Is the firm you plan to use insured? Professional associations insist their members are covered for both public and employer liability.

● Have you followed up references? Ask for the name of a previous satisfied customer and give them a ring, if you can't find a firm through personal recommendation. Your local authority may have a list of the companies it uses, and a blacklist.

● Get at least three estimates before choosing a firm. Then get a detailed quotation and check out all the prices involved (don't forget VAT) along with cancellation rights and guarantees.

● Get written confirmation of starting and finishing dates. Once a contract has been signed, failure to meet these deadlines could mean you have the right to cancel and get your money back, even if the job has been started.

● Are there any sub-contractors? If so, find out who will be responsible if things don't work out.

● Get a proper receipt with the contractor's name and address on it for any money handed over. If the company is not known to you, check out the address and phone number.

is best to pay by cheque or credit card, so you have some record of the payment. Don't pay the final instalment however, until you are satisfied that the job is completely finished, down to the last detail. That way your workers are less likely to disappear for weeks, leaving part of the job undone.

If things do go wrong, your first move is to write to the firm involved, asking them to put things right within a specified time. If this fails to produce results, contact your Citizens Advice Bureau or Trading Standards Office (via the town hall) for further help. You may be able to take the firm to the Small Claims Court if you feel you have been overcharged.

Interpreting advertisements

If no one knows of a suitable firm, it's time to consult local papers or telephone directories. Firms may display the symbol of an appropriate trade association which might give you some come-back if there are problems, but is not a guarantee of flawless work. It certainly pays to read between the lines when you're scanning the ads for a suitable firm.

'*Local firm*' Could be advertising the number of an agency many miles away who have a network of odd-jobbers throughout the suburbs. Prices are high because the workmen are charged commission by the agency for any work put their way.

'*Low hourly rates*' The firm will obligingly offer to come round in the evening, or on Saturday morning. What they do not tell you is that the rate then doubles, or even trebles.

'*No call-out charge*' These plumbers may have other ways of parting you from your money, such as making a 'special equipment' charge for using a pressure jet to unblock an outside drain that could have been cleared with a plunger.

'*Estimates given free*' Written quotations are not on offer.

Plumbing problems

One of the main complaints made about plumbers is that they charge excessively high prices, especially in emergencies, when people seldom work out the implications of an hourly rate. Even if you have an emergency, it's better to try and find a temporary solution to your problem and then start looking for the right firm to employ. Before you agree to pay a lot of money, find out if your emergency work can be done free. Some water boards still replace washers for nothing, for instance, and the local authority may deal with blocked drains.

There are simple steps you can take in an emergency to give yourself time to find a reputable plumber. If there is a leak:

● Turn off the water at the main stopcock.

● Turn off the immersion heater.

● Fill the bath with water. This drains the system, but keeps some water available.

● The toilet can be flushed by filling the cistern with a bucket.

● Keep some drinking water from the kitchen tap.

Wiring wisdom

Accidents with modern electrical systems and appliances are rare, but if your house is over 25 years old, it could be time for a re-wire. If you are moving to a new home, always get the wiring checked out by the Electricity Board, or by an electrician who is on the Roll of the National Inspection Council for Electrical Installation Contracting (NICEIC).

It isn't necessary to call out an electrician every time a fuse blows (see Know your own fuse box, page 98). However, if the same fuse goes more than once it deserves looking at, and any appliance that gives you an electric shock should be attended to promptly. Don't be tempted to tackle major electrical jobs yourself, and always take great care when dealing with minor problems:

● **Watch out** for sockets that feel any more than a little warm during use. Discolouring caused by heat around the pin holes is a danger sign.

● **Don't put** a 100 watt bulb into a fitting that specifies a maximum of 60.

● **Don't use** plugs that are broken, have gaps in the plastic cover or feel loose.

● **Never work** on a system that is live. Turn the power off before you touch any electrical repair, and don't turn it on again until you have completely finished.

● **Use** a tall, steady pair of steps when changing a bulb.

INDEX

ACKNOWLEDGEMENTS

Artists: *pages 38/39* Susan Robertson; *62/63* Val Hill
Additional copy: Christina Gregory

Photographic credits

Key HB: House Beautiful   EWA: Elizabeth Whiting Associates

Front cover Trevor Richards/HB; *back cover* Ian Kalinowski/HB; page *2* EWA; *3* HB; *6* EWA; *8/9* Ron Kelly/HB; *11* HB; *12* Lyndhurst by Texas Homecare; *13* Brian Harrison/HB; *15* HB; *16* HB; *17* Madeira from B & Q Heron Bathrooms; *18* Nocturne by Twyfords Bathrooms; *20* Albany by Twyfords Bathrooms; *21* EWA; *22* HB; *23* Ian Kalinowski/HB, HB; *25* Ian Kalinowski/HB *26* EWA; *27* Ron Kelly/HB; *28* Summer Oak by Stag Furniture; *31* EWA; *32* EWA; *33* EWA; *34* Trevor Richards/HB; *35* EWA; *36/37* Philips Lighting; *41* Tessarae from Dorma's Portfolio Collection; *42/3* Ashton Dean; *44* Geoffrey Frosh/HB; *45* Coloroll; *46/7* Coloroll; *48* EWA; *49* EWA; *51* both EWA; *52* small pic: Ashton Dean, large pic HB; *54* EWA; *55* EWA; *56* small pic: EWA, large pic: Galerie by Twyfords Bathrooms; *57* EWA; *58* Coloroll; *59* Garden Trail from Vymura's Country Diary range; *61* Coloroll; *65* Ian Kalinowski/HB; *66* Aspect by Doulton Bathroom Products; *66* Ron Kelly/HB; *71* Mr Tomkinson Crystal Twist range; *72* Mr Tomkinson Isadora 'Apricot'; *73* Mr Tomkinson Moresque; *75* EWA; *76* EWA; *77* EWA; *79* Ian Kalinowski/HB; *80* Sahara by Ashton Dean; *81* Tuliptime by Ashton Dean; *83* Coloroll; *84/85* HB; *96* EWA; *102/3* HB; *104* HB; *105* Ron Kelly/HB; *106* EWA; *107* Country Pine by Greaves and Thomas; *109* EWA; Roy Smith/HB; *110* Dominique by Ashton Dean; *111* EWA; *112* Calypso from the Dorma Metropolitan Collection, Blue Bows by Ashton Dean; *113* HB; *114* EWA; *115* Graham Rae/HB; *116* Jeremy Enness/HB; *117* Colin Poole/HB; *118* EWA; *119* Geneva from B & Q Heron Bathrooms; *120/121* Trevor Richards/HB; *122* Trevor Richards/HB; *123* Tom Leighton/HB; *124/125* EWA; *127* HB; *129* EWA; *130* EWA; *131* Galerie from Twyfords Bathrooms; *135* HB; *136/137* Farmhouse Pine by Hygena.